Slowenien **ARCHITEKTUR _ MEISTER & SZENE**
Slovenia **ARCHITECTURE _ THE MASTERS & THE SCENE**

Architektur im Ringturm XVII

Herausgeber | Editor Adolph Stiller

ARCHITEKTUR Slowenien
MEISTER & SZENE

Slovenia ARCHITECTURE
THE MASTERS & THE SCENE

VERLAG ANTON PUSTET

Diese Publikation erscheint anlässlich der gleichnamigen Ausstellung im Ausstellungszentrum der WIENER STÄDTISCHE Versicherung AG VIENNA INSURANCE GROUP in Wien, Schottenring 30.

This catalogue is publishd on the occasion of the exhibition of the same name at the exhibition center of the VIENNA INSURANCE GROUP in Vienna, Schottenring 30.

GESAMTKURATIERUNG | EXHIBITION CURATORS
Luka Skansi, Adolph Stiller

GRAFIK AUSSTELLUNGSTAFELN | GRAPHIC DISPLAY PANELS
studiobotas, Ljubljana

REDAKTION | EDITING
Adolph Stiller

KATALOG | CATALOGUE
ÜBERSETZUNGEN | TRANSLATION
aus dem Italienischen | from Italian: Erika Stiller-Lanz
aus dem Slowenischen | from Slovenian: Dr. Paul Apovnik
ins Englische | into English: Irma und Werner Rappl
LEKTORAT | COPY-EDITING
Deutsch | German: Erika Stiller-Lanz
Englisch | English: Irma Rappl-Wilson
GRAPHIC DESIGN
Haller & Haller, Wien
Paper: LuxoSamtoffset 150g
Cover: Alezan Cult 300g
Printing: TDS, Wien

© Fotos: lt. Angabe / as listed
© Texte bei den Autoren / Texts remains with the authors

ISBN 978-3-7025-0590-5

Kuratierung Ausstellungsteil | curators
exhibition part Edvard Ravnikar
Konzept | concept
Rok Žnidaršic, Majda Kregar, Miha Kerin
Mitarbeit | collaborator
Dejan Fortuna

Auswahl Archiv Architekturfakultät | Selection from archives FA
Miloš Kosec
Nejc Lebar
Žiga Misjak
Rok Žnidaršič

archives Ambient
Majda Kregar
Miha Kerin
Aleksander Bassin
Rok Žnidaršič

Archiv Architekturmuseum Ljubljana | archives AML
Bogo Zupančič
Martina Malešič
Rok Žnidaršič

Textauswahl | selection of texts:
Prof. Dr. Aleš Vodopivec
Mitarbeiter | collaborators:
Vid Kurinčič, Maša Ogrin

Planzeichnungen nach Originalen | plandrawings from the original:
Koordination | koordination Nejc Lebar
Mitarbeiter | collaborators:
Miloš Kosec, Žiga Misjak, Dejan Fortuna, Peter Plantan, Tina Krpan, Mojca Rebec, Denis Plahuta, Katja Pogačar, Katja Ložar, Urban Petranovič, Cilka Hosta, Ana Pezdirc
Digitalisierung und Grafik / digitalizing and graphic design:
Nika Grabar, Meta Zupančič, Tina Špat, Maša Ogrin

Unser besonderer Dank geht an folgende Personen und Institutionen, deren großzügige Unterstützung Ausstellung und Publikation ermöglicht haben:
We would like to especially thank the following people and institutions whose generous support made this exhibition and publication possible:

Friedrich Achleitner
Metka Dolenec
Zmaga Gale
Tadej Glažar
Miran Kambič
Stanko Kristl
Friedrich Kurrent
Milan Mihelič
Ana Porok
Aleš Vodopivec
Rok Žnidaršič
Maruša Zorec
Bogo Zupančič

Dank an alle Architekten, die an der Ausstellung teilnehmen.
Thanks to all architects, participating in the exhibition.

AML – Arhitekturni Muzej Ljubljana (Architekturmuseum Ljubljana | The Architectural Musem of Ljubljana)

Inhalt Contents

Slowenien ist ein Land vielfältiger landschaftlicher Schönheit. Von den Ausläufern des pannonischen Beckens über die Julischen Alpen reicht es bis hin zur mediterran geprägten Adriaküste, die liebevoll auch slowenische Riviera genannt wird. Die slowenische Architektur hat sich in diese Landschaft harmonisch eingefügt und sorgt für eine reizvolle Prägung.

Die Ausstellung und der dazu veröffentlichte Katalog bieten Einblicke in die reichhaltige Architektur dieses kleinen, und doch so bedeutsamen europäischen Landes. Die Architektur wird im Kontext mit der slowenischen Geschichte erfassbar gemacht und ermöglicht, die Schönheit und die historische Entwicklung zu erleben und zu begreifen.

Die Ausstellungsreihe *Architektur im Ringturm* widmet sich mit ihren Schwerpunkten der Architektur Zentral- und Osteuropas. Die VIENNA INSURANCE GROUP mit Sitz in Wien ist ein führender Versicherungskonzern in CEE und auch in Slowenien tätig. Unser Konzern ist grenzüberschreitend in insgesamt 23 Ländern dieser Region vertreten und wirtschaftlich erfolgreich. Mit der Ausstellungsreihe zur Architektur dieser Region laden wir zu einem Dialog ein, der Europa verbinden und die Menschen einander näherbringen soll.

Die architektonische Vielfalt unseres Nachbarlandes lässt sich durch eine Ausstellung und den Katalog nicht in ihrer ganzen Pracht und Bedeutung erfassen. Ich hoffe, dass wir bei vielen das Interesse zu einem Besuch in Slowenien geweckt haben. So kann die Publikation auch als architektonischer Reiseführer dienen, die Schönheit dieses gastfreundlichen Landes selbst zu erleben.

Vorwort Foreword

Slovenia is a country with a beautiful and varied landscape. It reaches from the edges of the Pannonian Basin to the Julian Alps all the way to the Adriatic coast characterized by a Mediterranean influence so that it is lovingly also called the Slovenian Riviera. Slovenian architecture is harmoniously integrated into this landscape and enhances its charm.

The exhibition and the accompanying catalogue offer insights into the rich architecture of this small and yet so important European country. The architecture is made understandable in the context of Slovenian history, making it possible to experience and grasp the beauty as well as the historical background.

The series of exhibitions *Architecture in the Ringturm* focuses on the architecture of Central and Eastern Europe. The VIENNA INSURANCE GROUP is a leading insurance group in CEE headquartered in Vienna and also does business in Slovenia. Our group is represented internationally in a total of 23 countries in this region and is financially successful. With a series of exhibitions on the architecture of this region we would like to initiate a dialogue bringing people closer together and connecting Europe.

The architectural variety of our neighbouring country in all its splendour and significance cannot be truly represented by a single exhibition and catalogue. So I hope that we have kindled a desire in many visitors to visit Slovenia. And the publication can also be used as an architectural guidebook for a first-hand experience of this beautiful, hospitable country.

Dr. Günter Geyer
Generaldirektor | General Manager
VIENNA INSURANCE GROUP

SLOWENIEN **MEISTER & SZENE**

Ausstellung und Publikation zeichnen Spuren nach und geben im übertragenen Sinn Kostproben des außergewöhnlich reichen baulichen Erbes, das ein so kleines Land wie Slowenien besitzt; es geht nicht darum, die komplette Geschichte der Architektur Sloweniens des 20. Jahrhunderts darzustellen. Die Publikation soll ein erster Begleiter sein und den neugierigen Reisenden – sei es nun der interessierte Historiker oder passionierte Architekt – anregen, sich einer bisher unbekannten architektonischen Kultur anzunähern.

Dieses Buch ist natürlich keineswegs eine komplette und treue Wiedergabe der slowenischen Architektur des 20. Jahrhunderts; zu viele sind die Schlüsselwerke und bedeutenden Realisierungen der Architektur, zu viele sind die Themen oder die kulturellen Einflüsse, die Slowenien in diesem Jahrhundert durchgemacht hat, um alles auf diesen Seiten zusammenzufassen. Die Ausstellung beschränkt sich auf 70 Projekte, ausgesucht auf der Basis einer kritischen Auswahl und historischen Bewertung – die schwierig und manchmal traumatisch ist – mit dem Ziel, so gut wie möglich die Komplexität, den Reichtum und eine weite Sicht der Architektur des 20. Jahrhunderts zu vermitteln.
Es ist klar, dass man dabei manchen Zwängen ausgesetzt ist: Zunächst im Hinblick auf die großen Meister der slowenischen Architektur wie Plečnik, Fabiani und Ravnikar, deren Bedeutung sich nicht nur auf ihre Arbeiten im Lande beschränkt. Sie werden durch einige zeichenhafte Werke dargestellt, unerwähnt bleiben muss die große Zahl ihrer außergewöhnlichen Werke, mit denen sie der slowenischen Stadt des 20. Jahrhunderts, oder wie im Falle von Fabiani, ganzen Teilen des Landes ihren Stempel aufgedrückt haben.

Ausstellung und Publikation
ARCHITEKTUR SLOWENIEN
Exhibition and publication
ARCHITECTURE SLOVENIA

Luka Skansi
Adolph Stiller

Ausstellungskommissäre
Exhibition Curators

This publication as well as the exhibition are following tracks and offering a 'taste' of the extraordinarily rich architectural heritage of a small country like Slovenia; it does not attempt to present a complete history of architecture of Slovenia in the 20th century; it is intended as an introductory companion for the curious visitor or traveller – interested historian or passionate architect – and hopes to encourage him or her to get acquainted with an as yet unknown architectural culture.
This book does not claim to be a complete and faithful account of 20th century Slovenian architecture; more key works and important examples of architecture, more subjects and cultural influences are to be found in Slovenia in this century than will fit on these pages. The exposition is restricted to 70 projects, chosen on the basis of a critical selection and historical evaluation – which was a difficult and sometimes traumatic process – aiming to render in the best possible way the complexity, abundance and farsightedness of 20th century architecture. This obviously involves facing some constraints: first with regard to the great masters of Slovenian architecture such as Plečnik, Fabiani and Ravnikar whose importance is not limited to their work in Slovenia. They are represented by several characteristic works; no mention can be made of the great number of extraordinary works with which they left their mark on the Slovenian city of the 20th century or on entire stretches of the country as in the case of Fabiani.

In diesem Sinne wird nun einem internationalen Publikum die Komplexität einer Reihe von „kleineren" Schauplätzen der Architektur präsentiert, geschaffen von Figuren, die parallel zu ihren großen Meistern und Lehrern ein ebenfalls erfolgreiches Berufsleben entwickelten. Mit dem Abstand der Jahre und aus dem Blickwinkel der wirtschaftlichen und politischen Bedingungen gesehen oder verglichen mit den nationalen und internationalen kulturellen Äußerungen der Zeit, ist deren Arbeit tatsächlich von großem Interesse. Ihre Arbeit erlaubt es, ein extrem heterogenes Bild der architektonischen Kultur Sloweniens zu zeichnen. Doch auch hier war man bestimmten Zwängen ausgesetzt: Um alle Architekten präsentieren zu können, wurden einige der grundlegendsten Arbeiten weggelassen sowie jene, die leider im Laufe der Zeit – aufgrund von gnadenlosen „Marktzwängen", aufgrund von einfachem Nicht-Wissen oder nicht zuletzt aufgrund von Barbarei – verschwunden sind.

Im Grunde sind es gerade diese Umstände, die einer Ausstellung über das Kulturgut eines Landes Bedeutung verleihen. Ein großes Publikum hat die Möglichkeit, das eigene Erbe kennenzulernen, den Reichtum und die Schönheit der historischen Schichtungen des physischen Raums, in dem es lebt, schätzen zu lernen. Der zeitgenössische Architekt kann sein Wissen über Architektur (heute leider im Durchschnitt eher gering) vertiefen und reflektieren im Zeitalter des medialen Konsums von Bildern, der auch die Architektur nicht verschont. Gemeinden, Regionen und ihre Vertreter können das Potential und die Bedeutung der Architektur für die Gestaltung des städtischen Raums ermessen. Ein architektonisch hochwertiges Gebäude beeinflusst das Aussehen, die Nutzung und die visuelle Ordnung der Stadt. Und in Slowenien gibt es gute Architektur in großem Umfang.

10

An international audience is now invited to view the complexity of a series of "minor" venues of architecture that were created by personalities who alongside their great masters and teachers likewise pursued successful professional careers. Seen from a distance in time and considering the economic and political conditions, their work is indeed of great interest compared with the national and international cultural statements of the time. Their work makes it possible to sketch an extremely heterogeneous image of the architectural culture of Slovenia. But also in this regard certain constraints had to be faced: in order to be able to present all the architects, it was necessary to leave out some of the most fundamental works as well as those which have unfortunately disappeared in the course of time – due to merciless "market constraints", to simple ignorance and last but not least, due to barbarism.

But this is exactly what makes an exhibition on the cultural assets of a country so important. A wide public is given the opportunity to become acquainted with its own heritage, to learn to appreciate the abundance and beauty of the historical layers of the physical space it lives in. The contemporary architect can deepen and reflect upon his knowledge of architecture (which today is unfortunately often quite limited), in an age of medial consumption of images which does not spare architecture either. Communities, regions and their representatives can assess the potential and the importance of architecture for the design of urban space. A building of high architectural value affects the appearance, the utilization and the visual organization of a city. And there is a great deal of good architecture in Slovenia.

In dieser Ausstellung soll das Augenmerk vor allem auf gute Architektur gelenkt werden. Das ist die einzige Möglichkeit, um sie wirklich kennenzulernen, und die Auswahl in diesem Buch reicht aus, um sie zu erleben, von allen Seiten zu betrachten, die Dimensionen, die Beziehungen zum Kontext zu erfassen und sie zu begreifen. Nur die physische Erfahrung des Gebäudes gibt seinen wahren Wert wieder. Und mit diesem Buch hoffen wir, das Interesse des Publikums von den bekannten, außergewöhnlichen landschaftlichen und historischen Qualitäten des Landes zusätzlich auf die Schönheit der alten und neuen Städte Sloweniens zu lenken.

Ausstellung und Katalog sind in drei Abschnitte geteilt, die die verschiedenen historischen und politischen Bedingungen Sloweniens im 20. Jahrhundert widerspiegeln: Der erste Teil widmet sich der Zeit zwischen den beiden Weltkriegen und entspricht einem Slowenien als Teil des jugoslawischen Königreiches (1918–1940), der zweite Teil befasst sich mit den Jahren des sozialistischen Jugoslawien (1945–1991), der dritte Teil umfasst Werke der jüngsten Entwicklung danach, infolge der Unabhängigkeit 1991. Jeder Abschnitt wird von einem Text eingeleitet, der einige wichtige Aspekte der Architekturdebatte, die wesentlichen kulturellen Ereignisse, den Reichtum an Werken und die Problematiken zusammenfasst.

In this exposition the main emphasis shall be on good architecture. This is the only way to really get to know it and the selection in this book is sufficient to experience it, look at it from all sides, to grasp and understand its dimensions and the relationship to the context. Only the physical experience of a building can actually convey its true value. And with this book we hope to direct the readers' interest from the well-known extraordinary scenic and historical qualities of the country also to the beauty of the old and new cities of Slovenia.

Exposition and catalogue are divided into three sections reflecting the different historical and political conditions in Slovenia in the 20th century: the first part is devoted to the period between the two world wars and corresponds to Slovenia as part of the Yugoslav Kingdom (1918–1940), the second part deals with the years of socialist Yugoslavia (1945–1991), the third part shows the latest developments after independence (1991). Each section is introduced by a text summarizing certain important aspects of the architectural debate, the main cultural events, the abundance of works and also the problems.

EIN STREIFZUG DURCH DIE SLOWENISCHE GESCHICHTE MIT WIEN-BEZUG
AN EXCURSION THROUGH THE HISTORY OF SLOVENIA IN CONNECTION TO VIENNA

FELIKS J. BISTER

Historiker | historian
Wien – Koper/Capodistra
Vienna – Koper/Capodistra

Die älteste Darstellung der Herzogseinsetzung
The earliest representation of the installation of the Dukes
aus | from: „Österreichische Chronik von den 95 Herrschaften"

Fragment aus den Freisinger Denkmälern
Fragment from the Freising Manuscripts
Bayrische Staatsbibliothek, München | Munich

Slowenien ist nach wie vor die Heimat der berühmten weißen Pferde, die mit ihrer Benennung als Lipizzaner den Namen des kleinen küstenländischen Weilers Lipica in die Kaiserstadt Wien und danach in die ganze Welt hinausgetragen haben. Ein Streifzug durch die slowenische Geschichte ist aber kein angenehmer Ritt auf dem Rücken eines stolzen Lipizzaners. Die Stürme der Zeit sorgten für sehr unterschiedliche Geschehnisse, wobei Krieg und Frieden oft eine verhängnisvolle Mischung eingingen. Die Slowenen selbst verwickelten ihre mächtigen nordwestlichen Nachbarn, die Baiern, sehr bald in heftige kriegerische Auseinandersetzungen, nachdem sie im 6. Jahrhundert „aus dem Dunkel der Geschichte" herausgetreten waren. Trotz der eher unfreiwilligen Bekehrung zum Christentum fand man später doch zum friedlichen Zusammenleben. Die Klostergründungen von Innichen (769) und Kremsmünster (777) markieren heute noch die damalige bairisch-karantanische Siedlungsgrenze, die man sich nicht als Schengengrenze vorstellen darf. Salzburg entsandte den Chorbischof *Modest* nach Maria Saal, dessen Kirche bis 1414 mit dem Fürstenstein bei Karnburg und dem Herzogstuhl auf dem Zollfeld den äußeren Rahmen für die besondere „in windischer Sprache" abgehaltene Zeremonie der Kärntner Herzogseinsetzung bildete. So wurde dieses Gebiet unter dem Mons Carantanus, dem heutigen Ulrichsberg, zu einer historischen Kernlandschaft, die für viele Slowenen immer noch das „slowenische Amselfeld" darstellt, worüber das Bundesland Kärnten nicht gerade glücklich ist.

Slovenia still is the home of the famous white horses called Lippizaner that carried the name of the small coastal village Lipica to the imperial city of Vienna and from there to the world. But an excursion through Slovenian history is no pleasure ride on the back of a proud Lipizzaner. The storms of time brought with them a very troubled sequence of events mixing war and peace in an often fatal way. The Slovenians themselves, after emerging from the darker periods of history in the 6th century, very soon involved their mighty north-western neighbours, the Bavarians, in heavy armed conflicts. In spite of their rather involuntary conversion to Christianity, peaceful cohabitation could later be established. The founding of the Monasteries of Innichen (769) and Kremsmünster (777) today still mark what at that time was the Bavarian-Carantanian border between settlements which one must not picture as a Schengen border. Salzburg sent off the Chorbishop *Modest* to Maria Saal whose church until 1414 together with the Prince's Stone near Karnburg and the Duke's Chair on the Zollfeld plain was the setting of the special ceremony of the installation of the Dukes of Carinthia which was held "in Slavic language". Therefore this area at the foot of the Mons Carantanus, today Ulrichsberg, became a historic centre, which for many Slovenians still is the "Slovenian Kosovo" – not exactly to the delight of the Federal Province of Carinthia.

Dem ehrgeizigen Missionswerk in Karantanien ist im 10. Jahrhundert die Entstehung der Freisinger Denkmäler zu verdanken. Sie stellen das älteste slawische Sprachdokument in lateinischer Schrift dar und sind somit ein Nachweis für die erste kulturelle Präsenz der Slowenen in Mitteleuropa. 500 Jahre später findet die slowenische Kultur durch die Reformation einen festen Platz in der europäischen Geistesgeschichte. Primus *Truber* (1508–1586), der slowenische *Luther*, dessen Lebensweg auch über Wien führte (1528), wurde neben seinen seelsorglichen Verdiensten zum Schöpfer der slowenischen Schriftsprache, da er 1550 die ersten slowenischsprachigen Bücher veröffentlichte – das *Abecedarium* und den *Catechismus* – sowie eine Reihe anderer Werke, darunter die Übersetzung des Neuen Testaments (1577). Im Jahr 1584 folgte die Übertragung der gesamten Heiligen Schrift ins Slowenische durch den protestantischen Schriftsteller und Theologen *Jurij Dalmatin* (1547–1589). Daher ist es verständlich, dass die selbstständige Republik Slowenien den Reformationstag zum Staatsfeiertag erklärte, obwohl das Land überwiegend katholisch ist.

Ebenso 1584 erschien auch die erste slowenische Grammatik *Arcticae horulae* von *Adam Bohorič* (1520–1598) in lateinischer Sprache. Seine Schreibweise, die *Bohoričica*, blieb etwa 250 Jahre in Gebrauch. 1592 folgte *Megisers* Wörterbuch *Dictionarium quatuor linguarum*, das in Graz herausgegeben wurde. Die eigentliche neuzeitliche Wende bringt jedoch erst

Primus Truber (1508–1586) – der
slowenische Luther | the Slovenian Luther
Holzschnitt von | woodcut by
Jacob Lederlein, 1578

14

Ambitious missionary work in Carantania in the 10th century is responsible for the creation of the Freising Manuscripts. They are the oldest existing document in Slavic language in the Latin alphabet and therefore proof of the first cultural presence of the Slovenians in Central Europe. 500 years later Slovenian culture finds its own place in European intellectual history through the Reformation. Primus *Truber* (1508–1586), the Slovenian *Luther* who also came to Vienna (1528) became, while also performing his pastoral duties, the father of the standard Slovenian language in that he published the first Slovenian books in 1550 – The *Abecedarium* and the *Catechism* – as well as a series of other works, including a translation of the New Testament (1577). In 1584, the translation of the entire Holy Bible into Slovenian by the protestant writer and theologian Jurij *Dalmatin* (1547–1589) followed. Therefore it is understandable that the independent Republic of Slovenia made Reformation Day a national holiday in spite of the fact that the country is predominantly Catholic.

In 1584, also the first Slovenian grammar was published: *Arcticae horulae* by Adam *Bohorič* (1520–1598), in Latin. His orthography, the Bohorič alphabet [Bohoričica] remained in use for approximately 250 years. In 1592, *Megiser's* Dictionary, the *Dictionarium quatuor linguarum*, edited in Graz, followed. The real turn towards modernity, strictly speaking, did not come until Marko's *Pohlin's Kraynska grammatika* (Ljubljana 1768), which in 1777 was quickly followed by *Windische Sprachlehre* by Ožbalt *Gutsman* (1725–1790), published in Klagenfurt, while the

Marko Pohlins Kraynska grammatika (Laibach 1768), der bereits 1777 die Klagenfurter Windische Sprachlehre von *Ožbalt Gutsman* (1725–1790) folgte, während 1808 der berühmte, in Wien tätige slowenische Slawist *Jernej (Bartholomäus) Kopitar* mit seiner *Grammatik der slavischen Sprache in Krain, Kärnten und Steiermark* für den einstweiligen Höhepunkt sorgte.

Bereits 1335 kamen nach der Steiermark (1282) auch die Kronländer Kärnten und Krain unter die habsburgische Herrschaft, Görz und Gradisca folgten 1500, während sich Triest 1382 freiwillig unter den Schutz des Herzogs *Leopold III.* von Österreich gestellt hatte. Dadurch befand sich nahezu das gesamte slowenische Volk im habsburgischen Länderkomplex. *Friedrich III.* zeigte sich an der von Slowenen bewohnten Region auch sehr interessiert. Seine berühmte Signatur A.E.I.O.U. (= Allen Ernstes ist Österreich unentbehrlich) ziert heute noch die Burg von Ljubljana. Der nicht gerade vom Schicksal begünstigte Kaiser gründete das Bistum Laibach (1462) und erteilte den Unterkrainern um Kočevje (Gottschee) 1492 die Erlaubnis zum Hausieren mit ihren Korbwaren etc. Dennoch blieb sein größter Widersacher, der Ungarnkönig *Matthias Corvinus* aus dem Geschlecht der Hunyadis bei den Slowenen als legendärer *Kralj Matjaž* in bleibender Erinnerung, obwohl *Reinhard Reimann* sich mit Recht darüber wundert, denn die Bewohner hatten unter den Plünderungen der ungarischen Söldnerheere nichts zu lachen. „König Matthias" wird in der Volksüberlieferung als *der* gerechte Herrscher geschildert,

famous Slovenian Slavonicist Jernej (Bartholomäus) *Kopitar* with his *Grammatik der slavischen Sprache in Krain, Kärnten und Steiermark*, presented a first highlight.

As early as 1335, after Styria (1282), also the crown estates of Carinthia and Carniola came under Habsburg rule, Gorizia and Gradisca followed in 1500, while Trieste had already voluntarily put itself under the protection of Duke *Leopold III* of Austria in 1382. Thus, almost the whole Slovenian people were integrated in the Habsburg complex of countries. *Frederick III* was also very interested in the region inhabited by the Slovenians. His famous signature A.E.I.O.U. (=Austria erit in orbe ultima) today still adorns the castle of Ljubljana. The emperor, who was not exactly favoured by fate, founded the diocese of Ljubljana (1462) and granted the inhabitants of Lower Carniola around Kočevje the permission to hawk their wickerwork, etc. Nevertheless, his greatest adversary remained the Hungarian King *Matthias Corvinu*s of the Hunyadi dynasty who is always well-remembered among the Slovenians as the legendary *Kralj Matjaž* although Reinhard *Reimann* is surprised, and rightly so, since the inhabitants really had a hard time when they were plundered by the Hungarian mercenary armies. In popular tradition, "King Matthias" is praised as *the* just king who became a central mythical figure as future "peacemaker and liberator". According to a Carinthian Slovenian legend, he is sitting with his warriors at a stone table on the Petzen in the Jaun Valley, waiting for his return, which will happen as soon as his beard has grown the seventh time around the

der als kommender „Friedensstifter und Befreier" eine zentrale mythische Figur geworden ist. Einer Kärntner slowenischen Sage nach wartet er mit seinen Kriegern in der Petzen im Jauntal bei einem steinernen Tisch sitzend auf seine Wiederkehr, die in dem Augenblick erfolgen wird, sobald sein Bart das siebente Mal um den Tisch gewachsen sein wird. Er wird dann der Gerechtigkeit zum Durchbruch verhelfen, was heutzutage nicht nur für Kärnten an der Zeit wäre. Offensichtlich galt *Matthias Corvinus* als mächtiger Beschützer der Landbevölkerung vor den zahlreichen Türkeneinfällen in Kärnten und Krain.

Das 16. Jahrhundert ist neben der Kirchenspaltung auch die Zeit der Bauernaufstände, obwohl es solche bereits vorher gegeben hat. Schon 1515 kam es auf Grund der großen Steuerbelastung, die sich wegen ständiger Kriegsführung ins Unerträgliche steigerte, wobei gleichzeitig die Verdienstmöglichkeiten eingeschränkt oder ganz unterbunden waren, zum großen Slowenischen Bauernaufstand, der in den innerösterreichischen Ländern von 80.000 Untertanen (Janko Prunk) unterstützt wurde. Im aus diesem Anlass in Wien gedruckten deutschsprachigen Flugblatt findet man die ersten slowenischen Worte, unter anderem „stara pravda" als Parole des Kampfes für das „alte Recht". Bekanntlich endeten die Angriffe der Bauern auf ihre Grundherren früher oder später mit empfindlichen Niederlagen, der große Kroatisch-slowenische Bauernaufstand 1572–1573, der tausende Opfer forderte, in einer blutigen Rache des Adels.

16

table. He will then help bring about justice, which would be necessary nowadays not only in Carinthia. Apparently, *Matthias Corvinus* was seen as a mighty protector of the rural population against the numerous Turkish invasions in Carinthia and Carniola.

The 16th century was not only the time of the schism, but also of peasants' revolts, although there had already been earlier ones. Already in 1515 when the high tax load caused by the permanent waging of war became unbearable and at the same time possibilities of earning an income were limited or entirely eliminated, the great Slovenian peasant revolt ensued, which in the Inner Austrian countries was supported by 80,000 subjects (Janko Prunk). On the leaflet which was printed in German on this occasion in Vienna, the first Slovenian words can be found, among others, "stara pravda" as the slogan of the fight for the "old law". As is well known, the peasants' revolts against their lords of the manor sooner or later ended with severe defeats, the great Croatian and Slovenian Peasant Revolt 1572–1573 which claimed thousands of victims ended in bloody retribution by the nobility.

As in the rest of Austria, also in the Slovenian countries the Counter-Reformation set a new course, since the Habsburg monarchs had already come to an agreement regarding the recatholisation of their population and at the same time banned Protestantism. The Peace of Augsburg Treaty "*cuius regio eius religio*" was implemented without exception.

Wie im übrigen Österreich setzte auch in den slowenischen Ländern die Gegenreformation neue Akzente, da sich die habsburgischen Landesherren schon 1579 über die Durchführung einer Rekatholisierung ihrer Bevölkerung geeinigt hatten, womit gleichzeitig der Protestantismus verboten wurde. Der Augsburger Beschluss „*Cuius regio eius religio*" wurde ausnahmslos realisiert. Nur in abgelegenen Tälern konnte der evangelische Glaube geheim praktiziert werden. Während der neu gegründete Jesuitenorden im 17. Jahrhundert im Zuge der Gegenreformation Gymnasien und höhere Schulen gründete, wofür er sich seitens des Kaisers eine Monopolstellung garantieren ließ, die eigentlich bis zur Auflösung des Ordens 1773 hielt, erfolgte parallel dazu die Verbrennung protestantischer Schriften. Dennoch ist es ein Faktum, dass mit der Errichtung des Jesuitenkollegs in Laibach im Jahre 1597 der Beginn des slowenischen höheren Schulwesens anzusetzen ist.

In der Habsburgermonarchie und ab 1867 im leider dualistisch geteilten Österreich-Ungarn erfuhren die Slowenen ihre politische und wirtschaftliche, in hohem Maß aber auch ihre kulturell-wissenschaftliche Prägung, wobei sie spätestens seit dem 15. Jahrhundert nicht nur Empfänger waren, sondern auch beachtliche Beiträge auf allen Wissensgebieten leisteten. Einige sollen namentlich genannt werden, so der Humanist Jurij (Georg) *Slatkonja* (1456–1522), der erste residierende Bischof von Wien (1513) und Begründer der Wiener Sängerknaben.

Georg (Jurij) Slatkonja
Erster residierender Bischof von Wien
First residing Bishop of Vienna
(1500–1522)

Only in secluded valleys could the Protestant faith be secretly practiced. While in the course of the Counter-Reformation in the 17th century the newly founded Jesuit Order was founding grammar schools and secondary schools for which purpose it had been granted a monopoly by the emperor which actually lasted until the dissolution of the Order in 1773, Protestant writings were being burnt. Nevertheless, it is an accepted fact that the construction of the Jesuit College in Ljubljana in 1597 marked the beginning of the Slovenian system of higher schooling.

As part of the Habsburg Monarchy and after 1867 in the unfortunately dualistically divided Austria-Hungary, the Slovenians received their political and economic, but to a large extent also their cultural-scientific formation whereby, since the 15th century at the latest, they were not only recipients, but also made considerable contributions in all fields of knowledge. Some are to be mentioned by name, for example the humanist Jurij (Georg) *Slatkonja* (1456–1522), the first residing Bishop of Vienna (1513) and founder of the Vienna Boys Choir. He called his fellow countryman, the versatile Augustinus *Tyfernus*, an architect and collector of antique inscriptions, to come to Vienna and build the Episcopal Palace for him. Thus *Tyfernus* alias *Prygl* was a predecessor of *Fabiani* and *Plečnik*. The polymath Bernard Perger (1440–1501) from the Stainz Valley in Lower-Styria was rector, dean and superintendent at the Alma Mater Rudolphina. In 1671, Lukas (Luka) *Knafelj*, the priest of Großrußbach, bequeathed by will his property to the university foundation in Vienna that was created in 1676 and named after him.

Er holte seinen Landsmann, den vielseitigen *Augustinus Tyfernus*, einen Architekten und Sammler antiker Inschriften nach Wien, der ihm den bischöflichen Palast erbaut hat. Demnach war *Tyfernus* alias *Prygl* ein früher Vorgänger von *Fabiani* und *Plečnik*. Als Rektor, Dekan und Superintendent wirkte der Polyhistor *Bernard Perger* (1440–1501) aus dem untersteirischen Stainztal an der Alma mater Rudolphina. Im Jahre 1671 vermachte der aus Unterkrain stammende *Lukas (Luka) Knafelj* als Pfarrer von Großrußbach sein Vermögen testamentarisch der 1676 errichteten und nach ihm benannten Universitätsstiftung in Wien. Weit über tausend, teils sehr bedeutende slowenische Dichter und Gelehrte zählten als Studenten zu ihren Nutznießern.

Im 18. Jahrhundert wirkten der Naturwissenschaftler und Germanist *Sigmund (Žiga) Popovič*, der schon erwähnte Sprachwissenschaftler *Marko Pohlin* und seit 1780 der berühmte Mathematiker und Astronom *Georg (Jurij) Vega* in Wien. *Vega* veröffentlichte das legendäre Logarithmisch-trigonometrische Handbuch, welches bis 1908 ansehnliche 82 Auflagen erreichte. In die Zeit der Kaiserin *Maria Theresia* fällt das verdienstvolle Wirken „des ersten österreichischen Bienenzuchtlehrers und Bienenforschers" *Anton Janša* (Janscha) aus Radovljica. Eine Gedenktafel im Augarten erinnert daran.

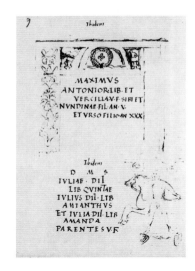

Zwei lateinische Inschriften
aus der Sammlung von
Two Latin inscriptions from the collection of
Augustinus Tyfernus
Österreichische Nationalbibliothek Wien,
Austrian National Library Vienna
CVP 3540

18

Far more than a thousand very important Slovenian poets and scholars benefited from it as students.

In the 18th century the natural scientist and Germanist, Sigmund (Žiga) *Popovič*, the linguist Marko *Pohlin* (mentioned above), and since 1780 the famous mathematician and astronomer Georg (Jurij) *Vega* worked in Vienna. Vega published the legendary logarithmic-trigonometric manual which until 1908 reached a considerable 82 editions. In the times of *Maria Theresa*, "the first Austrian apiarist and teacher of apiculture", Anton *Janša* (Janscha) from Radovljica, carried out his meritorious work. A commemorative plaque in the Augarten keeps his memory alive.

Vienna remains a particular centre of attraction for the Slovenian intelligentsia: Franz *Miklosich* (Miklošič) becomes the founder of Slavonic studies in Vienna. Before him (Jernej) *Kopitar*, author of the first scientific grammar of the Slovenian language mentioned earlier and amicable promoter of the creator of the Serbian standard language Vuk Stefanović *Karadžić* worked at the Imperial Court Library. The physicist Josef (Jožef) *Stefan*, the teacher of Ludwig Boltzmann, came from a Slovenian family living in Klagenfurt.

Naslovni list Janševega "Celotnega nauka o čebelarstvu", 1775.

Anton Janscha, 1775

Wien bleibt auch im 19. Jahrhundert ein besonderer Anziehungspunkt für die slowenische Intelligenz: *Franz Miklosich* (Miklošič) wird hier zum Begründer der Wiener Slawistik. Vor ihm wirkte an der Hofbibliothek *Bartholomäus (Jernej) Kopitar*, der Autor der bereits zitierten ersten wissenschaftlichen Grammatik der slowenischen Sprache und freundschaftliche Förderer des Schöpfers der serbischen Schriftsprache *Vuk Stefanović Karadžić*. Aus einer Klagenfurter slowenischen Familie stammte der Physiker *Josef (Jožef) Stefan*, der Lehrer von Ludwig Boltzmann.

In Wien studierten und lebten der slowenische Klassiker *France Prešeren*, der Schriftsteller sowie Literaturtheoretiker *Josip Stritar* und der größte Dichter der slowenischen Moderne *Ivan Cankar*, nach dem sogar eine Straße benannt wurde. Vor dem Ausbruch des Ersten Weltkriegs weilte für vier Monate der prominente Autor *Prežihov Voranc* (Lovro Kuhar) in Wien, wo er 1936 ruhigere Monate im Polizeigefängnis verbrachte. Die Wiener Zeit hat in ihrem Leben und Schaffen sichtbare Spuren hinterlassen, leider nicht nur angenehme.

Noch ein nicht unwesentliches Detail: Der „liberale" *Josef Zhisman* (Čižman) lehrte Kronprinz *Rudolf* mit offensichtlichem Erfolg praktische Toleranz, politische und religiöse Duldung, aber auch Opposition gegen die dominierenden Gesellschaftsschichten – Adel und Klerus.

The Slovenian classical author France *Prešeren* studied and lived in Vienna, as did the writer and literary theorist Josip *Stritar* and the greatest poet of Slovenian modernity, Ivan *Cankar*, after whom even a street is named. Before the outbreak of the First World War, the prominent author Prežihov *Voranc* (Lovro Kuhar) stayed in Vienna for four months where he later spent more quiet months in police prison in 1936. The time spent in Vienna left visible traces in his life and creativity, unfortunately not only pleasant ones.

Another not unimportant detail: the "liberal" Josef *Zhisman* (Čižman), taught Crown Prince *Rudolf* with apparent success practical tolerance, political and religious toleration, but also opposition to the dominating social classes – nobility and clergy.

The collapse of the monarchy put an end to the relationship of the Slovenians to Austria, which in the end was very tense. For their justified requests, such as the foundation of a Slovenian university, the 24 Slovenian delegates in the Vienna Reichsrat (Imperial Council) had in fact not succeeded in obtaining the support of the other nationalities, and even less that of the Imperial Governments, which were almost exclusively interested in "German vested rights". Therefore, the meetings of the leading Slovenian priest politician Anton *Korošec* (1872–1940) with Emperor Charles in October 1918, who once again offered a federalist transformation of Cisleithania, could only end with the symbolic phrase "*Your Majesty, it is too late*".

Der Zusammenbruch der Monarchie beendete das zum Schluss sehr angespannte Verhältnis der Slowenen zu Österreich. Es war nämlich den 24 slowenischen Abgeordneten im Wiener Reichsrat nicht gelungen, für ihre berechtigten Anliegen wie z.B. die Gründung einer slowenischen Universität, die Unterstützung der anderen Nationalitäten zu erhalten, noch weniger die der kaiserlichen Regierungen, die fast ausnahmslos auf den „deutschen Besitzstand" bedacht waren. So konnte das Gespräch des führenden slowenischen Priesterpolitikers *Anton Korošec* (1872–1940) mit Kaiser *Karl* im Oktober 1918, der darin nochmals eine föderalistische Umgestaltung Cisleithaniens anbot, nur mit dem sinnbildlichen *„Majestät, es ist zu spät"* enden. Die Weichen für eine „brüderliche" südslawische Zukunft waren längst gestellt. Obwohl die Erwartungen nach alldem, was man bereits als bitteren Vorgeschmack zu spüren bekam, nicht gerade rosig waren, wollte man einfach dem auch damals nicht allgemein verhassten „Völkerkerker" entfliehen, um ein Exempel zu statuieren. Die Slowenen überstanden die Zwischenkriegszeit im Ersten Jugoslawien dank der taktischen Klugheit ihrer unbestrittenen Führerpersönlichkeit *Korošec* verhältnismäßig gut. Schmerzhaft war durchwegs der Verlust eines Drittels ihres Siedlungsgebietes. Vor allem Italien wurde für den Übertritt an die Seite der Alliierten im Ersten Weltkrieg von diesen großzügig belohnt.

Österreichischer Reisepass von | Austrian passport of Korošec, Nr. | No. 1631, ausgestellt am | issued on 8. 5. 1917 vom Stadtrat Marburg | by the Marburg City Council

20

The way ahead, towards a "brotherly" South Slavic future had been pointed out long ago. In spite of the fact that after all the bitter foretaste that had already been experienced, expectations were not exactly rosy, the intention was simply also to escape the even then not generally hated "prison of nations" in order to set an example. Thanks to the tactical wisdom of their undisputed leader *Korošec*, the Slovenians survived the interwar period relatively well. The loss of a third of their settlement area was nevertheless painful. For its defection to the Allies in the First World War, especially Italy was generously rewarded.

In the Second World War, Nazi German ideology with its contempt for humanity and its war machinery, against which the majority of the Slovenians successfully defended themselves by joining Tito's partisan warfare, clearly represented an existential national threat. A small part collaborated with the Nazi occupiers which will for some time continue to make the reviewing of this historic period difficult. The heroic stories as well as the culprit and victim roles have to be verified by young historians without prejudice and judged anew, because until after Tito's death in 1980, the dictatorial communist regime of the post-war period did not allow an open discussion.

Eine eindeutig existenzielle nationale Bedrohung bedeutete der Zweite Weltkrieg mit der nazideutschen menschenverachtenden Vernichtungsideologie und Kriegsmaschinerie, gegen die sich die Slowenen mehrheitlich mit dem Anschluss an Titos Partisanenkampf erfolgreich wehrten. Ein kleinerer Teil kollaborierte mit der Nazibesatzung, was die Aufarbeitung dieses historischen Abschnitts noch länger erschweren wird. Die Heldengeschichten sowie die Täter- und Opferrollen müssen alle von jüngeren Historikern vorurteilsfrei geprüft und neu beurteilt werden, denn das diktatorische kommunistische Regime der Nachkriegszeit erlaubte erst nach Titos Tod 1980 eine offene Diskussion.

Mit der überraschenden Wende durch den Zerfall Jugoslawiens und der Gründung der unabhängigen Republik Slowenien am 25. Juni 1991 ist die Möglichkeit der demokratischen und freien Meinungsäußerung gegeben, die auch voll wahrgenommen wird, erfreulicherweise auch im kulturellen Leben und in der wissenschaftlichen Forschung. Mit dem gestiegenen Selbstbewusstsein präsentiert sich heute die kleine slowenische Nation in vieler Hinsicht einfach großartig!

The unforeseen turn of events headed off by the collapse of Yugoslavia and the foundation of the independent Republic of Slovenia on June 25th, 1991, offered the possibility of democratic and free expression of opinion which is being fully taken advantage of, fortunately also in cultural life and in scientific research. With increased self-confidence, the small Slovenian nation in many ways presents itself today as simply great!

DIE ARCHITEKTUR DER ERSTEN HÄLFTE DES 20. JAHRHUNDERTS IM SLOWENISCHEN RAUM
Vom Architekten Anton Laščak bis zu den Schülern Plečniks bei Le Corbusier
ARCHITECTURE ON SLOVENIAN AREA DURING THE FIRST HALF OF THE 20TH CENTURY
From the architect Anton Laščak to the students of Plečnik with Le Corbusier

BOGO ZUPANČIČ
Kustos im Architekturmuseum Ljubljana
Curator at the Museum of Architecture in Ljubljana

Ivan Vurnik
Kooperative Handelsbank
Cooperative Commercial Bank
Ljubljana 1921–22
Kassenhalle | counter hall

Dynamik und Komplexität kennzeichnen die Architektur im Raum der heutigen Republik Slowenien in der ersten Hälfte des 20. Jahrhunderts. Sie ist im Rahmen der damaligen gesellschaftlichen Kräfte und Kunstströmungen zu sehen, die sich zwischen den örtlichen Besonderheiten wie auch den nationalen bis hin zu den internationalen Stilpräferenzen bewegten. Das behandelte Thema umfasst die Zeit vom Ende des 19. Jahrhunderts bis zum Ende des ersten Weltkrieges im Rahmen der österreichisch-ungarischen Monarchie, die Zeit nach dem ersten Weltkrieg im Staat der Serben, Kroaten und Slowenen bzw. im Königreich Jugoslawien – aber auch das Geschehen im Küstenland, im damaligen östlichen Randgebiet des Königreiches Italien, blieb doch ein Teil des slowenischen ethnischen Territoriums bis zur Kapitulation Italiens außerhalb des Gebietes des Mutterlandes. Vom Erdbeben in Ljubljana zu Ostern des Jahres 1895 bis zum Beginn des zweiten Weltkrieges entwickelte sich die Architekturdiskussion immer mehr zu einer Auseinandersetzung zwischen Traditionalismus und Moderne.

Slowenische Intellektuelle in technischen Berufen, die vorwiegend in Wien in deutscher Sprache ausgebildet wurden, gab es Ende des 19. Jahrhundert – einschließlich der Architekten – sehr wenig. Das erste Buch in slowenischer Sprache, das die spezifische Terminologie der Architektur einführt, trägt den Titel „Stavbinski slog" (Der Baustil), wurde im Jahre 1885 vom Geistlichen Janez Flis verfasst und diente kirchlichen Zwecken.

Dynamics and complexity characterize architecture in the area of today's Republic of Slovenia in the first half of the 20th century. This architecture has to be seen in connection with the social forces and artistic trends of that time which were situated between local and national particularities as well as international preferences in style. The subject at hand encompasses the period from the late 19th century to the end of World War I within the Austro-Hungarian Monarchy, the time after World War I as part of a nation of Serbs, Croatians and Slovenians and within the Kingdom of Yugoslavia – but also the events in the coastal area, in the eastern border zone of the Kingdom of Italy of that time, as, after all, part of the Slovenian ethnic territory remained on the other side of the mother country's boreders until the capitulation of Italy. In the period between the earthquake in Ljubljana at Easter 1895 to the beginning of World War II, the architectural discussion increasingly turned into a confrontation between traditionalism and modernity.

Slovenian intellectuals in technical professions who were educated mainly in Vienna, in the German language, were very rare in the late 19th century – including architects. The first book in the Slovenian language that introduces the specific terminology of architecture is entitled "Stavbinski slog" (Architectural Style) was written in 1885 by the clergyman Janez Flis and was used for ecclesiastical purposes.

Die bedeutendsten slowenischen Kunsthistoriker[1] und Architekten[2] dieser Zeit wurden in Wien ausgebildet, unter ihnen setzten sich in Wien vor allem die beiden Architekten Max Fabiani (1865–1962) unter anderem mit dem Palais des Möbelhauses Portois & Fix und Jože Plečnik (1872–1957) mit dem Zacherl-Haus durch. Architekten und Baumeister, die in Ljubljana vor und nach dem Erdbeben 1895 bauten, waren neben einer kleinen Zahl von Slowenen vor allem Deutsche, Friulaner, Tschechen und Kroaten, einige Architekten waren gemischter ethnischer Herkunft, wie z.B. Max Fabiani, Josip Costaperaria (1876–1951) und Ciril Metod Koch (1867–1925). Am Ende des 19. und zu Beginn des 20. Jahrhunderts setzte sich im Zuge der Erneuerungsarbeiten nach dem Erdbeben der Stil der Sezession durch, etwas später wurde unter dem Einfluss der Politik die Suche nach einem nationalen Stil in die Architektur hineingetragen. Einige Architekten suchten – aus unterschiedlichen Gründen – Gelegenheiten, außerhalb der Grenzen des damaligen Staates zu arbeiten, z.B. Ivan Jager (1871–1959), der in Minneapolis in den USA und Anton Laščak (1846–1946), der in Ägypten, in der Türkei und in Italien wirkte. Jager war nationalbewusst und suchte nach einem slowenischen Nationalstil, nicht so jedoch der etwas ältere Laščak[3]. Seine Villa im neoislamischen Stil mit dem Park auf dem Rafut bei Gorica (Görz), im Jahre 1909 entworfen, wirkt noch heute wie eine Architektur-Fatamorgana.

Josef Plečnik
Zacherlhaus | Zacherl House
Wien | Vienna 1903–05

The most important Slovenian art historians[1] and architects[2] of that time were educated in Vienna, and among them were particularly the two architects, Max Fabiani (1865–1962), who, with the palace of the furniture store Portois & Fix, among other buildings, and Jože Plečnik (1872–1957), with the Zacherl-House, gained acceptance in Vienna. Architects and master builders building in Ljubljana before and after the earthquake of 1895 were, with the exception of a small number of Slovenians, especially Germans, Friulians, Czechs and Croatians, and some architects were of mixed ethnic origin such as Max Fabiani, Josip Costaperaria (1876–1951) and Ciril Metod Koch (1867–1925). In the late 19th and early 20th century the Secessionist style gained acceptance in the course of the reconstruction work after the earthquake, and a short time after that, under the influence of politics, architecture began to search for a national style. Some architects sought – for different reasons – opportunities to work outside of the borders of the national territory of that time, e.g. Ivan Jager (1871–1959) who worked in Minneapolis in the USA and Anton Laščak (1846–1946) who worked in Egypt, Turkey and Italy. Jager was nationally conscious and tried to create a Slovenian national style, quite different from the slightly older Laščak[3]. His villa on the Rafut near Gorica, designed in 1909, today still appears like an architectural fata morgana.

1 Das waren France Stelé (1886–1972), Izidor Cankar (1886–1958) und Vojeslav Mole (1886–1973).
2 Zu diesen zählen die Architekten Max Fabiani, Ivan Jager, Jože Plečnik und Ivan Vurnik.
3 Der Görzer Architekt Anton Laščak (auch Antonio Lasciac) schloss sich der italienischen Elite an und kam mit ihrer Hilfe und auch durch glückliche Umstände zu Aufträgen am ägyptischen Königshof. Zwischen 1882 und 1886 wirkte er in Alexandria und zwischen 1897 und 1939 in Kairo. Er plante viele Paläste, sein umfangreiches Opus enthält u. a. auch eine koptische Kirche und ein Museum im islamischen Stil in Kairo sowie den Plan für eine Synagoge in Rom. Seine Arbeiten pendeln stilistisch zwischen den Ansprüchen der Auftraggeber und sezessionistischen, neoklassischen und neuislamischen Stilvarianten. Laščak wurde Mitglied der Accademia Nazionale di San Luca in Rom und wurde mit dem Adelstitel Beg ausgezeichnet, in der slowenischen Fachwelt ist er jedoch völlig unbekannt.

Max Fabiani
Portois & Fix
Wohn- und Geschäftshaus |
residential and commercial building
Wien | Vienna 1899–1900

Max Fabiani
Volkshaus | House of the People
Triest 1905

1　These were France Stelé (1886–1972),
　　Izidor Cankar (1886–1958) and
　　Vojeslav Mole (1886–1973).
2　These include the architects Max
　　Fabiani, Ivan Jager, Jože Plečnik and
　　Ivan Vurnik.
3　The Gorizian architect Anton Laščak
　　(also Antonio Lasciac) joined the
　　Italian elite and with their help and also
　　fortunate circumstances was awarded
　　contracts at the Egyptian royal court.
　　Between 1882 and 1886 he worked in
　　Alexandria and between 1897 and 1939
　　in Cairo. He designed many palaces,
　　his extensive oeuvre includes among
　　other things a Coptic church and a
　　museum in Islamic style in Cairo as
　　well as the draft for a synagogue in
　　Rome. The style of his works oscillates
　　between his customers' demands and
　　Secessionist, Neoclassical and Neoisla-
　　mic variants. Laščak became a member
　　of the Accademia Nazionale di San
　　Luca in Rome and was awarded the title
　　of nobility Beg, but in the Slovenian pro-
　　fessional world he is entirely unknown.

Die größte und am besten entwickelte slowenische Stadt in der Zeit der österreichisch-ungarischen Monarchie war die multiethnische Hafenstadt Triest mit einem starken slowenischen Hinterland. In Triest bildeten sich allmählich slowenische Institutionen heraus, z.B. der Narodni dom (Volkshaus) aus dem Jahre 1905, ein Bauwerk des Architekten Max Fabiani und die Schule der Gesellschaft der hl. Kyrill und Methodius bei Sv. Jakob aus dem Jahre 1912, eine Arbeit des Architekten Josip Costaperaria, zu den in dieser Zeit entstandenen Institutionen kann auch Fabianis Trgovski dom (Haus der Wirtschaft) in Gorica (Görz) aus dem Jahre 1905 gezählt werden. Die Bestrebungen der slowenischen Elite, Triest zu einem nationalen Mittelpunkt zu machen, wurden nach dem Zerfall des österreichisch-ungarischen Kaiserreiches und der raschen Besetzung eines Teiles des slowenischen ethnischen Territoriums zunichte gemacht. Das Volkshaus „Narodni dom" in Triest und andere slowenische Institutionen im Küstenland wurden bald darauf Ziele italienischer faschistischer Exzesse.

Einen markanten Wendepunkt in der Entwicklung der slowenischen Architektur brachte der Zerfall der österreichisch-ungarischen Monarchie und die Gründung des neuen gemeinsamen Staates der Serben, Kroaten und Slowenen 1918 sowie der Universität in Ljubljana 1919, die zur Wirkungsstätte neuer Generationen slowenischer Architekten wurde, mit neuen Ideen aber auch Gegensätzen. Von Wien kehrten die bereits erwähnten Kunsthistoriker nach Ljubljana

The biggest and best developed Slovenian city at the time of the Austro-Hungarian Monarchy was the multi-ethnic seaport of Trieste with a strong Slovenian hinterland. In Trieste, Slovenian institutions gradually began to take shape, e.g. the Narodni Dom (House of the People) of 1905, a building by the architect Max Fabiani and the School of the Society of the Saints Cyril and Methodius near Sv. Jakob in Trieste of 1912, a work by the architect Josip Costaperaria, also Fabiani's Trgovski Dom (House of Economy) in Gorica of 1905 can be counted among the institutions created at that time. The efforts of the Slovenian elite to make Trieste a national centre were shattered after the fall of the Austro-Hungarian Monarchy and the rapid occupation of part of Slovenian ethnic territory. The House of the People, "Narodni dom", in Trieste and other Slovenian institutions in the coastal area soon became targets of fascist Italian excesses.

A striking turning point in the development of Slovenian architecture was the fall of the Austro-Hungarian Empire and the foundation of a new common nation of Serbs, Croatians and Slovenians in 1918 as well as the foundation of the university in Ljubljana in 1919, which became the sphere of activity of new generations of Slovenian architects, with new ideas, but also differences. The art historians mentioned above returned from Vienna to Ljubljana, the architect Ivan Vurnik (1884–1971) was entrusted with the setting up a department of architecture at the university of Ljubljana.

zurück, der Architekt Ivan Vurnik (1884–1971) wurde mit der Einrichtung einer Abteilung für Architektur an der Universität Ljubljana betraut. Vurnik wollte für die Ausbildung der zukünftigen Architekten sowohl Max Fabiani aus Wien wie auch Jože Plečnik, der seit 1911 in Prag lehrte, heranziehen. Architekt Fabiani widmete sich dem Wiederaufbau der zerstörten Goriška (Provinz Görz), daher kehrte er in sein heimatliches Štanjel zurück, während Plečnik die Einladung annahm. Das Ziel der nationalbewussten slowenischen Elite war es, die provinzielle Stadt Ljubljana zum nationalen Zentrum umzuformen. Die Suche nach einem nationalen Stil bei Vurnik und anderen slowenischen Architekten war daher ein zentrales Thema der Architektur, das sich in Arbeiten wie der Zadružna gospodarska banka (Kooperative Handelsbank) und dem Sokolski dom na Taboru (Haus der Sokolen) in Ljubljana manifestiert. Plečnik war neben seiner Lehrtätigkeit in Ljubljana noch mit der Neugestaltung des Hradschin in Prag im Auftrag des Staatspräsidenten T. G. Masaryk stark in Anspruch genommen, daher konnte er zu Beginn und in der Mitte der zwanziger Jahre in Ljubljana keine größeren Projekte beginnen. Ivan Vurnik gab den Nationalstil auf, nachdem er 1925 die Internationale Kunstgewerbe- und Industrieausstellung in Paris gesehen hatte und sich dem Funktionalismus anschloss. Ab dem Jahre 1926, als sich die Professoren Vurnik und Plečnik zerstritten, wurden die Gegensätze zunehmend größer. Etwa in dieser Zeit kehrten nach Beendigung ihrer Studien im Ausland junge slowenische Architekten[4] nach Ljubljana zurück. Diese bildeten gemeinsam mit den

For the training of the future architects Vurnik wanted to call in both Max Fabiani from Vienna and Jože Plečnik, who had been teaching in Prague since 1911. The architect Fabiani devoted himself to the reconstruction of the destroyed Goriška (Province of Goricia), and therefore returned to his native Štanjel, while Plečnik accepted the invitation. The goal of the nationally conscious Slovenian elite was to remodel the provincial city of Ljubljana to become the nation's centre. Therefore, the search for a national style was a prerogative of Vurnik's and other Slovenian architects' architecture, formulated in works like the Zadružna gospodarska banka (cooperative bank of economy) and the Sokolski dom na Taboru (House of the Sokols) in Ljubljana. Besides teaching in Ljubljana, Plečnik was also busy redesigning the Hradčany in Prague by order of the President T. G. Masaryk, therefore he could not take on any bigger projects in Ljubljana in the early and mid-20s. Ivan Vurnik abandoned the national style after seeing the International Exposition of Modern Industrial and Decorative Arts in Paris in 1925 and joined functionalism. After 1926, when the professors Vurnik and Plečnik had fallen out, the differences increased. At about the same time young Slovenian architects[4] were returning to Ljubljana after they had completing their studies abroad. Together with Vurnik's students and those dissatisfied with Plečnik's seminar they formed a modernist and yet discriminating opposition to Plečnik's understanding of architecture, which in the time of increasing modern tendencies was anachronistic and yet optimally met the objectives of extension of the national metropolis.

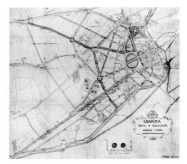

Max Fabiani
Regulierungsplan | Regulation plan
Gradisca 1920

Max Fabiani
Haus Hribar | Hribar house
Ljubljana 1905–06

4 Architekt Vladimir Mušič (1893–1973) erwarb das Diplom 1922 an der Technischen Hochschule in Wien, Architekt Vladimir Šubic (1894–1946) beendete sein Studium 1922 an der deutschen Technischen Hochschule in Prag, der avantgardistische Künstler Avgust Černigoj (1898–1985) war 1923 im Bauhaus in Weimar, Architekt Ivo Spinčič (1902–1985) beendete sein Studium 1925 bei Prof. Peter Behrens an der Akademie in Wien, Architekt Josip Costaperaria erwarb sein Diplom 1927 im Alter von 51 Jahren bei Prof. Clemens Holzmeister in Wien.

4 The architect Vladimir Mušič (1893–1973) acquired his diploma in 1922 at the University of Technology in Vienna, the architect Vladimir Šubic (1894–1946) completed his studies in 1922 at the German University of Technology in Prague, the avant-garde artist Avgust Černigoj (1898–1985) was in 1923 member of the Bauhaus in Weimar, the architect Ivo Spinčič (1902–1985) completed his studies in 1925 with Prof. Peter Behrens at the Academy of Fine Arts in Vienna, the architect Josip Costaperaria earned his diploma in 1927 at the age of 51 with Prof. Clemens Holzmeister in Vienna.

Ivan Vurnik
Kooperative Handelsbank
Cooperative Commercial Bank
Ljubljana 1921–22

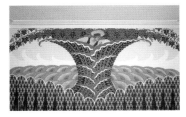

Josip Costaperaria
Villa Perhavec
Ljubljana 1932

Heute Zentrale der slowenischen Lehrergewerkschaft
Restaurierung durch Bevk-Perović arhitekti
Now Labour Union of Teachers of Slovenia, head office
Restoration by Bevk-Perović arhitekti

Studenten Vurniks und den Unzufriedenen aus der Plečnik-Schule eine modernistische, doch differenzierte Opposition gegen Plečniks Architekturverständnis, das in der Zeit zunehmender moderner Tendenzen ein Anachronismus war, dem Ziel des Ausbaues der nationalen Metropole jedoch bestens entsprach. Der Funktionalismus war in der Zeit zwischen 1925 und 1933 im Aufwind, was auch die avantgardistische Zeitschrift Tank (1927) und die Zeitschrift Arhitektura (1930–34) beweisen, für die auch Architekten aus Zagreb und Beograd schrieben, sowie das Buch Stanovanje (Die Wohnung) der Architekten Ivo Spinčič und Jože Mesar (1931). Eine bedeutende Wende in der Mitte der zwanziger Jahre stellt die Anlehnung des Slowenentums, das wegen der geographischen Nähe traditionell unter deutschem Einfluss stand, an die französische Kultur dar, obwohl zahlreiche slowenische Architekten in Wien und Prag studierten[5]. Ab dem Jahre 1925 wurden Stipendien der französischen Regierung ausgeschrieben, die unter den Architekten als erster Dušan Grabrijan (1899–1952), ein Diplomand Plečniks, in Anspruch nahm (und sich während seines Studiums an der Ecole des Beaux-Arts in Paris mit der modernen Architektur „infizierte"). Nach 1930 widmete er sich der pädagogischen und publizistischen Arbeit in Sarajevo. Die dem Funktionalismus huldigenden Architekten arbeiteten jeder für sich und unorganisiert, obwohl einige Mitglieder der Gruppe „Petkovci" waren. Diese Gruppe bildeten im Ausland ausgebildete Vertreter der modernen Architektur wie Costaperaria, Spinčič und Stanko Rohrman (1899–1973), bekehrte Diplomanden Plečniks,

Ivo Spinčič
Villa Kobi
Ljubljana, Barje

29

5   Zu ihnen zählen die Architekten Ivo Medved (1902–1974), der sein Studium 1928 an der Technischen Hochschule in Wien abschloss, Jože Mesar (1907–2002), der sein Studium 1930 bei Behrens beendete, Jože Sivec (1896–1974) beendete 1932 das Studium in Wien, Ljubo Humek (1913–1988) erwarb sein Diplom 1938 an der Technischen Hochschule in Prag.

5   These include the architects Ivo Medved (1902–1974), who completed his studies in 1928 at the University of Technology in Vienna, Jože Mesar (1907–2002), who completed his studies in 1930 with Behrens, Jože Sivec (1896–1974) completed his studies in Vienna in 1932, Ljubo Humek (1913–1988) acquired his diploma in 1938 at the German University of Technology in Prague.

In the time between 1925 and 1933, functionalism was on the up and up which is also confirmed by the avant-garde journal Tank (1927) and the journal Arhitektura (1930–34) with contributions also by architects from Zagreb and Beograd as well as by the book Stanovanje (The Appartment) by the architects Ivo Spinčič and Jože Mesar (1931). An important event in the mid-20s was that Slovenian identity, which, due to geographic proximity had traditionally been under German influence, began to depend more on French culture, in spite of the fact that many Slovenian architects (probably because of the proximity) studied in Vienna and Prague[5]. Since 1925, the French government had been offering scholarships which Dušan Grabrijan (1899–1952), one of Plečnik's diploma students, was the first among the architects to accept (and during his studies at the Ecole des Beaux-Arts in Paris become "infected" by modern architecture). After 1930, he devoted himself to pedagogical and journalistic work in Sarajevo. The architects following functionalism worked each on his own and outside of organisations, although some were members of the "Petkovci" group. This group included representatives of modern architecture who had received their education abroad, such as Costaperaria, Spinčič and Stanko Rohrman (1899–1973), converted diploma students of Plečnik, such as France Tomažič (1899–1968) and Maks Strenar (1901–1968), furthermore renegades of Plečnik's seminar, who later earned their diploma with Vurnik: Herman Hus (1896–1960), Janko Omahen (1898–1980), Domicijan Serajnik (1899–1983).

z.B. France Tomažič (1899–1968) und Maks Strenar (1901–1968), weiters Abtrünnige aus der Plečnik-Schule, die später bei Vurnik ihr Diplom machten: Herman Hus (1896–1960), Janko Omahen (1898–1980), Domicijan Serajnik (1899–1983). Der älteren Generation der Funktionalisten gelang es nicht, sich im professionellen Umfeld duchzusetzen und einen entscheidenden Einfluss auf das Geschehen im Lande zu bewirken. Plečnik bekam immer mehr und immer größere Aufträge im Städte- wie auch Sakralbau – obwohl bei den ersteren auch nicht alles glatt ging; den Funktionalisten aber blieben nur private Aufträge etwa für Wohnblocks und Villen am Stadtrand. In Ljubljana wurden in den dreißiger Jahren von Costaperaria der Wohnblock „Šahovnica" (Das Schachbrett) und einige Villen auf der Vrtača errichtet, nennenswert sind weiters die „Dukič-Wohnsiedlung" von Sivec und Villen von Šubic, Rohrman, Strenar, Spinčič, Mušič und Tomažič. Wie man moderne Tendenzen und zeitgenössische technische Errungenschaften erfolgreich mit der klassischen Fassade verbinden und dabei einen Mittelweg einschlagen kann, zeigte der Architekt Vladimir Šubic mit dem „Nebotičnik" (Wolkenkratzer) in Ljubljana (1930–33), der für kurze Zeit sogar das höchste Gebäude in Mitteleuropa war. Bei diesem neuen Bautyp orientierte er sich zweifellos an der amerikanischen Architektur. Die erste Generation der Plečnik-Schüler und die Abtrünnigen aus seinem Seminar brachen nicht völlig mit Plečniks Überlieferung, weil es einfach wegen der Gegebenheiten und des Niveaus der Auftraggeber nicht zu radikaleren Veränderungen kommen konnte, was man ihren Arbeiten auch

Maks Strenar
Villa Maria Vera
Ljubljana 1929

Josip Costaperaria
Villen in der Levstikova-Straße
Villas in Levstikova Street
Ljubljana 1929–32

30

The older generation of functionalists did not succeed in gaining acceptance in the professional environment and in exerting a decisive influence on the events in the country. Plečnik was awarded increasingly more and bigger orders in urban development and sacred building – although not everything went smoothly in urban development; but for the functionalists only private orders were left, for example, for apartment houses and villas on the outskirts of the city. In Ljubljana, Costaperaria built the apartment house "Šahovnica" (the chessboard) and some villas on the Vrtača in the 30s, also worthy of mention are furthermore the Dukič housing estate by Sivec and villas by Šubic, Rohrman, Strenar, Spinčič, Mušič and Tomažič. How modern tendencies and contemporary technical achievements could be successfully combined with the classical façade thereby steering a middle course was demonstrated by the architect Vladimir Šubic with the "Nebotičnik" (skyscraper) in Ljubljana (1930–33) which for a short time was even the highest building in Central Europe. With this type of building he was doubtlessly oriented towards American architecture. The first generation of Plečnik students and the renegades of his seminar did not completely break with Plečnik's tradition because the circumstances and the culture of the customers did not allow for more radical changes which shows verymuch in their work. Outside of the centre they could be somewhat more modern, see for example the buildings of Plečnik's two diploma students Saša Dev (1903–1967) and Jaroslav Černigoj (1905–1989) in Maribor, as well as of the Behrens student and Le Corbusier trainee Franc Novak in the Prekmurje area.

Josef Plečnik
Friedhof | cemetery Žale
Ljubljana um | around 1937

ansieht. Etwas moderner konnten sie außerhalb des Zentrums sein, so bauten etwa die beiden Plečnik-Diplomanden Saša Dev (1903–1967) und Jaroslav Černigoj (1905–1989) in Maribor und der Behrens-Student und Le Corbusier-Praktikant Franc Novak in der Region Prekmurje.

Die Hinwendung zu traditionelleren Tendenzen in der Architektur erfolgte nach dem Jahre 1933 und fiel zeitlich teilweise mit der Wirtschaftskrise und dem Attentat auf den jugoslawischen König Alexander in Marseille Ende 1934 zusammen. In diese Wende fällt auch die Affäre um den Wettbewerbsentwurf für die National- und Universitätsbibliothek, in der sich als Protagonisten Plečnik und Vurnik gegenüber standen und Vurnik letztlich erfolglos blieb. Die neue Zeitschrift „Kronika slovenskih mest" (Chronik der slowenischen Städte), 1934–1940, widmete historischen und slowenischen Themen mehr Aufmerksamkeit. Plečnik realisierte ab Ende der zwanziger Jahre zahlreiche Bauten in Ljubljana, u. a. das Gebäude der Versicherungsgesellschaft „Vzajemna" (1928–30), die Tromostovje (Drei Brücken, 1931–32); die National- und Universitätsbibliothek (1936–41), den Allerheiligen-Garten (1938–40), die Schleusen (1939–45) und die Markthallen (1940–42). Die jüngeren Generationen der Plečnik-Diplomanden waren angesichts der zunehmenden Informationen über den Architekten Le Corbusier, die Brüder Perret und andere zeitgenössische Architekten und Tendenzen immer unzufriedener mit Plečniks Beharren auf den traditionalistischen Standpunkten in der Architektur, daher wünschten sie sich Kontakte mit dem Ursprung der modernen Architektur selbst. In den dreißiger Jahren gingen gleich neun

Jaroslav Černigoj, Aleksander Dev
Sparkasse der Provinz Drava
The Drava Province Savings Bank
Maribor 1930–31

The change of direction towards more traditional tendencies in architecture happened after the year 1933, and partly coincided with the economic crisis and the assassination of the Yugoslavian King Alexander in Marseille at the end of 1934. At the time of this turn of events also the of competition project affair for the national and university library took place, a showdown between Plečnik and Vurnik in which Vurnik finally lost. The new journal "Kronika slovenskih mest" (Chronicle of the Slovenian Cities), 1934–1940, focussed on historical and Slovenian topics. From the late 20s on, Plečnik carried out many buildings in Ljubljana, among others, the "Vzajemna" insurance company building (1928–30), the Tromostovje (Tripple Bridges),1931–32; the National and University Library (1936–41), the All-Saints-Garden (1938–40), the sluices (1939–45) and the market halls (1940–42).
Due to increasing information on the architect Le Corbusier, the Perret brothers and other contemporary architects and tendencies, the younger generations of Plečnik diploma students were increasingly discontent with Plečnik's insistence on traditional attitudes in architecture and therefore wanted contacts with the origin of modern architecture itself. In the 30s, nine Slovenians and one Serb from the Vojvodina who studied with Plečnik all at once went to the guru of architecture in Paris, making up a considerable contribution to the total number of young architects from all over the world who were allowed to learn at the studio in the Rue de Sèvres[6]. In Le Corbusier's studio some came to know the works of Charlotte Perriand, others became acquainted with Japanese and Danish architects, e.g. Nielsen and Ejnar Borg,

6 The first Slovenian and Plečnik diploma student to visit the studio of Le Corbusier and Pierre Jeanneret in the Rue de Sèvres in Paris, was the architect Miroslav Oražen (1900–1975) i.e. in the year 1929. He spent the school year 1930/31 on a French government scholarship at this studio, in 1933/34 he was followed by Milan Sever, and in summer 1938 by the Behrens student Franc Novak (1906–1959). In the school year 1938/39 even four Plečnik diploma students stayed with Le Corbusier: Hrvoje Brnčič (1914–1991), Marjan Tepina (1913–2004), Jovan Krunić (1915–2001) and in spring 1939 also Edvard Ravnikar. In 1939/40 he was followed by Jovan Krunić (for a second time) and Marko Župančič (1914–2007).

Slowenen und ein Serbe aus der Vojvodina, der bei Plečnik studierte, zum *Guru der Architektur* nach Paris, was in der Gesamtzahl der jungen Architekten aus aller Welt, die im Atelier in der Rue de Sèvres arbeiten durften, einen beträchtlichen Anteil ausmacht[6]. In Le Corbusiers Atelier lernten einige die Arbeiten von Charlotte Perriand kennen, andere wurden mit japanischen und dänischen Architekten bekannt, z.B. Tage Nielsen und Ejnar Borg, mit denen sie die Kontakte auch später aufrechterhielten. Die sieben Plečnik-Diplomanden, die bei Le Corbusier praktizierten, markieren demnach schon Ende der dreißiger Jahre die Abkehr von den Arbeitsprinzipien Plečniks, gleichzeitig aber stehen sie für die Kontinuität der Denkweise in der Architektur (einschließlich jener von Plečnik), die sie aus den ausgehenden dreißiger Jahren in die vierziger und fünfziger Jahre hinüberbrachten. Mit Wettbewerbsbeiträgen etwa von Sever, Tepina und Ravni-

6 Der erste Slowene und Plečnik-Diplomand, der das Atelier von Le Corbusier und Pierre Jeanneret in der Rue de Sèvres in Paris besuchte, war der Architekt Miroslav Oražen (1900–1975) und zwar im Jahre 1929. Als Stipendiat der französischen Regierung verbrachte er auch das Schuljahr 1930/31 in diesem Atelier, ihm folgte 1933/34 Milan Sever und im Sommer 1938 der Behrens-Student Franc Novak (1906–1959). Im Schuljahr 1938/39 waren gleich vier Plečnik-Diplomanden bei Le Corbusier: Hrvoje Brnčič (1914–1991), Marjan Tepina (1913–2004), Jovan Krunić (1915–2001) und im Frühjahr 1939 noch Edvard Ravnikar. Diesem folgten 1939/40 Jovan Krunić (ein zweites Mal) und Marko Župančič (1914–2007).

32

Marko Župančič
„Haus für einen Architekten"
"Villa for an architect"
Ljubljana um | around 1940

with whom they also maintained contact later. In this way, in the late 30s, Plečnik's seven diploma students already marked their break with Plečnik's working principles, but at the same time they stand for the continuity of the way of thinking in architecture (including that of Plečnik) which they carried forth from the late 30s to the 40s and 50s. With competition entries for example by Sever, Tepina and Ravnikar, with drafts, e.g. that of Župančič for an architect's villa and also with the first works such as the Moderna galerija by Ravnikar, they became part of the animated architectural arena of that time, brought new vigour to it and showed possibilities for change. The architect Edvard Ravnikar becomes the key figure of the architectural scene after World War II, and the ensuing changes in society. Many architects support the reconstruction of their home country which had been destroyed during the war, but Edvard Ravnikar succeeds in winning acceptance at the university where he could create a platform for further work and development by reshuffling the professorial staff. But this is already the beginning of a new chapter in the Slovenian history of architecture.

kar, mit Entwürfen, z.B. jenem von Župančič für eine Architektenvilla und auch mit den ersten in Angriff genommenen Realisierungen, etwa der Moderna galerija von Ravnikar, wurden sie Teil der damaligen lebendigen Architekturszene, gaben dieser neuen Elan und zeigten Wege für Veränderungen auf. Schlüsselfigur des Architekturgeschehens nach dem zweiten Weltkrieg und den damit verbundenen gesellschaftlichen Veränderungen wird der Architekt Edvard Ravnikar. Viele Architekten setzen sich für die Erneuerung der im Krieg zerstörten Heimat ein, doch Edvard Ravnikar gelingt der Durchbruch an der Universität, wo er durch einige Umbesetzungen in der Professorenschaft eine Plattform für die weitere Arbeit und Entwicklung schaffen konnte. Hier beginnt allerdings schon ein neues Kapitel der slowenischen Architekturgeschichte.

Jože Plečnik
in seinem Arbeitszimmer | in his study
Ljubljana, um | around 1940

Marjan Tepina, Le Corbusier
Aufnahme vermutlich von Edo Ravnikar,
der zur selben Zeit in der rue de Sèvres
arbeitete
Picture probably taken by Edo Ravnikar,
working at the same time in the office
rue de Sèvres
um | around 1939

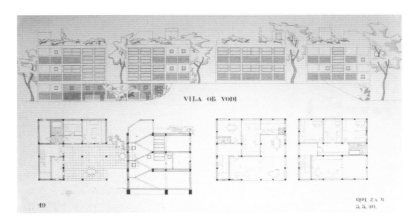

Marko Župančič
„Haus am Fluss"
"Villa by the river"
Ljubljana 1940

Ivan Vurnik
Haus der Sokolen (Rote Falken) |
House of the Sokols,
Turnhalle | gymnasium
Ljubljana 1923–27

Vladimir Šubic
„Nebotičnik", Wolkenkratzer | skyscraper
Ljubljana 1930–33

Vladimir Šubic
„Grafika"-Gebäude | "Grafika" Building
Ljubljana 1937

Jože Plečnik
„Vzajemna" Versicherung | Insurance company
building
Ljubljana 1928–30

Jože Plečnik
National- und Universitätsbibliothek
National and University Library
Ljubljana 1931–41

Edvard Ravnikar
Galerie der Moderne
The Modern Gallery
Ljubljana 1939–51

40

Jože Plečnik
Dreibrücken | Triple Bridge 1930–31
Markt | The Market 1940–42
Ljubljana

Jaroslav Černigoj, Aleksander Dev
Sparkasse der Provinz Drava
The Drava Province Savings Bank
Maribor 1930–31

Herman Hus
Der kleine Wolkenkratzer
The Small Skyscraper
Ljubljana 1931–32

Vladimir Mušic
„Roter Wohnhof" | "Red House"
Council Apartment Complex
Ljubljana 1927–29

Jaroslav Černigoj, Aleksander Dev
Wohnblock Gradišče (früher Hutter-Block) | Housing
Block Gradišče (formerly Hutter's Housing Block)
Maribor 1939–41

Vladimir Šubic
Meksika Wohnanlage | apartment complex
Ljubljana 1926–27

Jože Plečnik
Christi-Himmelfahrtskirche
Parish Church of the Ascension
Bogojina 1924–27, 1950–56

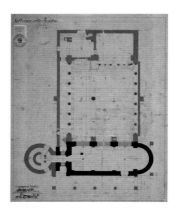

Jože Plečnik
Kirche St. Michael im Laibacher Moor
Church of St. Michael in the Marsh
Ljubljana-Barje 1925, 1937–38

France Tomažič
Villa Oblak
Ljubljana 1931–35

Maks Strenar
Villa Maria Vera
Ljubljana 1929

Stanislav Rohrman
Villa Neuberger
Ljubljana 1930–31

Josip Costaperaria
Villen in der Levstikova-Straße und
„Schachbrett"-Wohnhaus |
villas in the Levstikova Street and
"Chessboard" Apartment Building
Ljubljana 1929–32

France Tomažič
Villa Grivec
Ljubljana 1934–36

DIE SLOWENISCHE ARCHITEKTUR 1945-1980
Edvard Ravnikar und seine Schule
SLOVENIAN ARCHITECTURE 1945-1980
Edvard Ravnikar and his school

ALEŠ VODOPIVEC

Architekt und Professor an der Architekturfakultät
Architect and professor at the faculty of architecture
Ljubljana

Die slowenische Architektur der zweiten Hälfte des 20. Jh. ist durch die Arbeit und die Ideen Edvard Ravnikars geprägt, der sich schon bald nach dem Ende des Zweiten Weltkrieges mit einer Reihe von Wettbewerbssiegen als zentrale Fachautorität im gesamten damaligen Jugoslawien durchgesetzt hat. Ravnikar war Plečniks hervorragendster Schüler und nach Beendigung seines Studiums noch zwei Jahre sein engster Mitarbeiter bei der Erstellung der Ausführungspläne für das Gebäude der National- und Universitätsbibliothek in Ljubljana. Im Jahre 1939 ging Ravnikar nach Paris, wo er mehrere Monate bei Le Corbusier arbeitete. Nach Kriegsende wurde er Professor an der Abteilung für Architektur der damaligen Technischen Fakultät in Ljubljana. Mit Bauobjekten, Projekten, engagierter publizistischer Arbeit und vor allem mit seinem pädagogischen Charisma prägte Ravnikar nachhaltig die slowenische Architektur, den Städtebau, aber auch das Design. Auf die herausragende Bedeutung Ravnikars machte bereits die Ausstellung „Neuere slowenische Architektur 68"[1] aufmerksam, waren doch von den 65 in der Ausstellung gezeigten Arbeiten nicht weniger als 50 von Ravnikar und seinen Diplomanden.

Von einer slowenischen Architektur können wir zwar erst nach 1921 reden, als die erste heimische Architekturschule gegründet wurde, war doch bis dahin die Bautätigkeit in der Hand fremder Entwerfer und Bauunternehmer. Es ist die Zeit des Zerfalls der österreichisch-ungarischen Monarchie, und die Slowenen glaubten, dass die Fremdherrschaft zu Ende sei.

Edvard Ravnikar
Revolutionsplatz
Square of the Revolution
Ljubljana 1960–82

Slovenian architecture in the second half of the 20th century was greatly influenced by the works and ideas of Edvard Ravnikar who soon after the end of World War II, after winning a series of competitions, gained acceptance as a central authority of architecture throughout Yugoslavia. Ravnikar was Plečnik's most outstanding student and after finishing his studies remained for two years his closest collaborator while preparing the construction drawings for the National and University Library in Ljubljana. In 1939, Ravnikar went to Paris where he worked for several months with Le Corbusier. After the end of the war he became professor at the Department of Architecture of what at that time was the Faculty of Technology in Ljubljana. With built objects, projects, his writings and above all with his pedagogical charisma, Ravnikar had a long-lasting influence on Slovenian architecture, urban development and also design. Ravnikar's exceptional importance had already been demonstrated in the exposition "New Slovenian Architecture 68"[1], since not less than 50 of the 65 works presented in the exposition were by Ravnikar and his diploma students.

Slovenian architecture came into its own only after 1921, when the first national school of architecture was founded, because until then building activities had been in the hands of foreign designers and building contractors. The Austro-Hungarian Monarchy was disintegrating and Slovenians believed that the era of foreign rule had come to an end. It was also the general public mood of national awareness at that time that inspired Plečnik to look for a national identity in architecture.

1 Novejša slovenska arhitektura '68, Zveza arhitektov Slovenije, Ljubljana 1968 (Neuere slowenische Architektur '68, Verband der Architekten Sloweniens)

1 Novejša slovenska arhitektura '68, Zveza arhitektov Slovenije, Ljubljana 1968 (New Slovenian Architecture '68, Association of Architects of Slovenia)

Die allgemeine Stimmung der nationalen Euphorie ließ damals auch Plečnik nach einer nationalen Identität in der Architektur suchen.

Plečnik war kein Anhänger einer nationalen Romantik und sah daher keine Notwendigkeit, einen slowenischen Stil zu erfinden. Er suchte den Charakter oder den Ausdruck, der unserem geographischen Raum entspricht: „Es geht um den Ausdruck, den ihr überall seht. Schaut euch nur eine deutsche Stadt an, sofort erkennt ihr, dass sie deutsch ist, sofort erkennt ihr die Note, die für sie charakteristisch ist."[2] Nach Ravnikars Worten hat Plečnik „die slowenische Architektur nach dem Süden umorientiert. Ohne Plečniks Wirken hätte die slowenische Architektur nicht ihre eigentümliche Farbe, die auch Bestandteil unserer kulturellen Physiognomie ist"[3]. Ravnikar wies darauf hin, dass uns eigentlich erst Plečnik lehrte, die heimischen kulturellen Werte zu schätzen.

In diesem Sinne interessierte sich auch Ravnikar für die elementare Kraft der Volksarchitektur, die „dem Suchen der gegenwärtigen Architektur erstaunlich nahe ist"[4]. Ebenso intensiv beschäftigte sich Ravnikar mit der modernen Architektur und Kunst wie auch mit ihrer Vergangenheit: nicht nur mit unserem Baukulturerbe, sondern auch mit der Geschichte der Kunst, Kultur, Philosophie und allgemeinen Geschichte. Kurzum, auch Ravnikar erforschte unsere Kultur im Lichte der Suche nach der Identität der zeitgenössischen slowenischen Architektur. Nicht zuletzt

54

Plečnik was no supporter of national romanticism and therefore saw no need to invent a Slovenian style. He looked for a character or an expression that would correspond to our geographic region: "What is important is what you see expressed everywhere. You only have to look at a German town, you immediately recognize that it is German, immediately recognize its characteristic note."[2]. According to Ravnikar, Plečnik "reoriented Slovenian architecture towards the south. Without Plečnik's work Slovenian architecture would not have its peculiar colour which is also part of our cultural physiognomy"[3]. Ravnikar pointed out that only Plečnik actually taught us to appreciate our own cultural values.

In this sense, also Ravnikar was interested in the elementary force of popular architecture which "comes amazingly close to the quest of contemporary architecture"[4]. With equal intensity, Ravnikar dealt with modern architecture and art as well as with their past: not only with our architectural heritage, but also with the history of art, culture, philosophy and history in general. In short, also Ravnikar investigated our culture searching for the identity of contemporary Slovenian architecture. Last but not least, he was also interested in archaeology in order to discover the logic of space in the depth of older layers. Thorough research of the wider surroundings and of the characteristics of a more restricted locality are Ravnikar's points of departure in his search for the corresponding architectural concept. That is why his architecture is such a unique synthesis of the modern and the traditional, of the universal and the local.

2 Dušan Grabrijan, Plečnik in njegova šola (Plečnik und seine Schule), Obzorja, Maribor 1968, Seite 76
3 Edo Ravnikar, Architekt Jože Plečnik 76 letnik, (Architekt Jože Plečnik 76 Jahre), Slovenski poročevalec IX, Ljubljana 1948 (24.1.), Nr. 20
4 Edo Ravnikar, Sedem naglavnih grehov naše arhitekture (Die sieben Hauptsünden unserer Architektur), Sodobnost, Ljubljana 1963, Nr. 10, Seite 924

2 Dušan Grabrijan, Plečnik in njegova šola (Plečnik and his school), Obzorja, Maribor 1968, page 76
3 Edo Ravnikar, Architekt Jože Plečnik 76 letnik, (Architect Jože Plečnik 76 years), Slovenski poročevalec IX, Ljubljana 1948 (24.1.), No. 20
4 Edo Ravnikar, Sedem naglavnih grehov naše arhitekture (The seven deadly sins of our architecture), Sodobnost, Ljubljana 1963, No. 10, page 924

interessierte er sich für die Archäologie, um in der Tiefe älterer Schichten die Logik des Raumes zu entdecken. Die gründliche Erforschung des weiteren Umfeldes und die Charakteristika der engeren Örtlichkeit sind für Ravnikar Ausgangspunkt bei der Suche nach der entsprechenden architektonischen Konzeption. Daher ist seine Architektur eine so eigenständige Synthese des Modernen und Traditionellen, des Universellen und Ortsgebundenen.

Der Schlüssel für das Verstehen der Architektur Ravnikars ist der Hallentrakt des im Jahre 1960 errichteten Amtsgebäudes der Gemeinde Kranj. Diese Arbeit bedeutete ohne Zweifel die Abwendung vom dogmatischen Modernismus der internationalen Regeln, bringt sie doch die einheimische Tradition in ihrer Verbindung mit der modernen Architektursprache zum Ausdruck. Es handelt sich nicht um eine typisch moderne Arbeit, um ein autonomes Objekt im Raum, sondern um einen örtlich angepassten Modernismus, um eine Architektur mit einer erkennbaren kulturellen Identität des Umfeldes.

Ungeachtet der verhältnismäßig bescheidenen Ausmaße unterteilte er den geplanten neuen Trakt in mehrere Bauobjekte, die den offenen Raum umschließen. Es entstand eine Piazzetta mit einem Hallenobjekt, das die Raumachse visuell bestimmt. In der Gestaltung des Gebäudes ist sowohl der Einfluss Plečniks bzw. der Semperschen Bekleidungstheorie als auch der Einfluss Le Corbusiers, d.h. der englisch-französischen Tradition offensichtlich, die die Authentizität des Baustoffes und die Autorität der Konstruktion in den Vordergrund stellt. Die originäre,

The key to understanding Ravnikar's architecture lies in the Community Hall of the municipality of Kranj, built in 1960. This work doubtlessly meant an abandonment of the dogmatic modernism of international rules since it expresses the national tradition in its connection with the modern language of architecture. It is not a typically modernist work, an autonomous object in space, but a locally adapted modernism, architecture with a recognizable cultural identity of the environment.

Regardless of the relatively modest dimensions, he divided the new wing into several buildings enclosing the open space. A piazzetta with a hall object visually determining the spatial axis was created. The design of the building clearly reveals the influence of Plečnik and of Semper's "theory of dressing" as well as the influence of Le Corbusier, i.e. of the English-French tradition emphasizing the authenticity of the building material and the authority of the structure. The original, three-dimensionally shaped structure as a special feature of the contemporary art of engineering is the basic guideline both of the spatial concept and of the articulation of the outer appearance of the building object. The visible structure determines the proportions, the rhythm and the dimensions of the building. Its front is axially symmetrical, an unconventional paraphrase of the classical temple. The actual volume of the building is raised. The roof floats on top in form of a folded plate. In the contemporary conception and modern structure we find traces of popular architecture: the saddleback roof, a logical structure, the use of indigenous building materials, modest and well thought-out details, simple organization

Edvard Ravnikar
Stadthalle | Municipal Hall
Kranj 1954–60

plastisch geformte Konstruktion, als besondere Qualität der zeitgenössischen Ingenieurkunst, ist die grundlegende Richtschnur sowohl des Raumkonzeptes als auch der Artikulation des äußeren Erscheinungsbildes des Bauobjektes. Die sichtbare Konstruktion bestimmt die Proportionen, den Rhythmus und die Maße des Baues. Seine Stirnfront ist achsensymmetrisch, eine eigenwillige Paraphrase des klassischen Tempels. Das eigentliche Volumen des Gebäudes ist angehoben. Darüber schwebt das Dach in Form einer gefalteten Platte. In der zeitgenössischen Konzeption und modernen Konstruktion sehen wir Spuren der Volksarchitektur: das Satteldach, eine logische Konstruktion, die Verwendung heimischer Baumaterialien, bescheidene und durchdachte Details, eine einfache Gliederung des Innenraumes und eine verhaltene Feierlichkeit. Historische, schon vergessene und neu entdeckte Motive, Konstruktionsprinzipien und Raumkonzepte, in Kombination mit Grundsätzen der Moderne, schaffen eine Architektur, die außerordentlich in den Raum eingewurzelt ist.

Ravnikar verwies auf die Aussagekraft und das künstlerische Potential der abstrakten Sprache der modernen Architektur vor allem mit der Gestaltung von Gedenkstätten zur Erinnerung an die Opfer des zweiten Weltkrieges (Rab, Draga, Begunje u.a. 1952–53). Diese stehen in diametralem Widerspruch zur monumentalen Figuralität der Denkmäler in den damaligen Ländern des Ostblocks. Mit dem Ende des sowjetischen Einflusses auf Jugoslawien im Jahre 1948 fand auch der sozialistische Realismus in der jugoslawischen Kunst verhältnismäßig früh sein Ende.

Edvard Ravnikar
Gedenkstätte | Memorial Draga
Draga 1952-53

of the inner space and a subtle but festive aura. Historical, almost forgotten and newly discovered motives, structural principles and spatial concepts combined with modernist principles create a type of architecture that is deeply rooted in the region.

Ravnikar emphasized the expressiveness and artistic potential of the abstract language of modern architecture, particularly in the design of memorials for the victims of World War II (Rab, Draga, Begunje a.o. 1952–53). These are diametrically opposed to the monumental figurality of the monuments in the countries of the Eastern Block at that time. With the end of Soviet influence in Yugoslavia in 1948 also Socialist Realism in Yugoslavian art came to a relatively early end. Nevertheless, Ravnikar's projects are in our country the first messengers of abstract art which in painting and sculpture could find acceptance only in the late 50s. The Mediterranean character of our architecture which is determined by the specific climatic and topographic features of the area, the typical vegetation, the local building materials, the logic of traditional building and the people's customs had already been discovered by Plečnik. This trait also distinguishes Ravnikar's projects, e.g. the draft of a complex of holiday apartments in the Karst (1946–47) that was never built, with the typical stone walls surrounding the traditional courtyard, the so-called "borjač" which served to provide protection from the Bora.

Dennoch sind Ravnikars Projekte die ersten Boten der abstrakten Kunst bei uns, die sich in der Malerei und Bildhauerei erst gegen Ende der fünfziger Jahre durchsetzen konnte.

Den mediterranen Charakter unserer Architektur, der durch die klimatischen und landschaftlichen Besonderheiten, durch die typische Vegetation, die örtlichen Baumaterialien, die Logik der traditionellen Bauweise und die Lebensgewohnheiten der Menschen bestimmt ist, hat schon Plečnik entdeckt. Dieser Charakter zeichnet aber auch Ravnikars Projekte aus, z.B. den Entwurf für eine nicht realisierte Feriensiedlung im Karst (1946–47), mit den typischen Steinmauern um den traditionellen Hof herum, der sogenannten „Borjač", die Schutz vor der Bora bietet. Noch mehr trifft dies auf seinen Vorschlag für eine völlig neue, moderne Stadt an der Grenze zu Italien zu – Nova Gorica (1948–50; offensichtlich unter dem Einfluss von Le Corbusier konzipiert), oder das mit dem ersten Preis ausgezeichnete Wettbewerbsprojekt für den Fremdenverkehrskomplex Sv. Štefan – Miločer – Pržno (1964): Der Ausgangspunkt der städtebaulichen Konzeption sind die landschaftlichen Besonderheiten des montenegrinischen Küstenlandes – die Erhaltung und Ergänzung der Baum- und Weinrebenkulturen, sodass sie sich in unregelmäßigen Formen der reich gegliederten Topographie anpassen und sich die Aussicht über die Bepflanzung hinweg auf den Meereshorizont öffnet.

Das Bauen in der Stadt ist für Ravnikar vor allem eine Herausforderung, wie man die neue, moderne Architektur mit der bestehenden städtischen Struktur in Einklang bringt. Eine selbst-

58

This is even more true for his proposal of an entirely new modern city on the border to Italy – Nova Gorica (1948–50; obviously inspired by Le Corbusier) or the competition project for the tourism complex Sv. Štefan – Miločer – Pržno (1964), which won first prize: the point of departure of the urban planning concept is the particular landscape of the Montenegrin coastal area, the conservation and completion of the tree and vine cultures so that they adapt in irregular shapes to the very differentiated topography opening the view from over the tops of the plants to the horizon on the sea.

For Ravnikar, building in the city represents above all the challenge of reconciling new modern architecture with the existing town structure. He rejected a self-sufficient "egocentric" type of architecture. In 1960 he won the competition for the Trg revolucije (today Trg republike) complex in Ljubljana, which was to shape the new city centre. At the same time, this centre was supposed to also symbolically mark the square of the capital of the republic. He proposed three independent building objects which resolved the complex situation of a larger area connecting the historic complex of the former monastery with a church on one side with several pre-World War II residential buildings on the other side. He marked the so-called "Ljubljana Gate" with two high-rise buildings (this name gained acceptance in the course of time due to the particular geographic position of the city between two hills), a kind of symbolic portal; he separated the historic environment of the monastery complex from the new monumental square with a horizontally incorporated long rectangular block of masonry.

Edvard Ravnikar
Gedenkstätte Konzentrationslager Kampor
Kampor Concentration Camp Memorial
Rab (Kroatien | Croatia) 1953

Edvard Ravnikar
Gedenkstätte Konzentrationslager Kampor
Kampor Concentration Camp Memorial
Rab (Kroatien | Croatia) 1953

5 10   50m

genügsame, „egozentrische" Architektur lehnte Ravnikar ab. Im Jahre 1960 gewann er den Wettbewerb für den Komplex Trg revolucije (heute Trg republike) in Ljubljana, der dem neuen Stadtzentrum Form geben sollte. Zugleich sollte dieses Zentrum auch symbolisch den Platz der Hauptstadt der Republik markieren. Sein Vorschlag löste mit drei eigenständigen Bauobjekten die verworrene Situation eines größeren Raumes, in dem der historische Komplex des ehemaligen Klosters mit der Kirche auf der einen Seite an mehrere Wohngebäude aus der Zeit vor dem Zweiten Weltkrieg auf der anderen Seite anschließt. Mit zwei Hochhäusern markierte er das sogenannte „Laibacher Tor" (dieser Name setzte sich in der Geschichte wegen der besonderen geographischen Lage der Stadt zwischen zwei Hügeln durch), eine Art symbolisches Portal, mit einem horizontal verlegten langen Quaderstein trennte er das historische Ambiente des Klosterkomplexes vom neuen monumentalen Platz.

In der unmittelbaren Nachbarschaft wies Ravnikar mit dem Wohnkomplex „Ferant-Garten" (1964–76) auf die Bedeutung der historischen Bauweise der Jahrhundertwende und der traditionellen offenen Räume in einem Wohnviertel hin – mit Hofflächen auf der einen Seite und Straßen auf der anderen Seite. Das bestehende Straßennetz machte er zum Ausgangspunkt der neuen Grenzbebauung (bis an den straßenseitigen Parzellenrand). Auf diese Weise schuf er eine zeitgenössische Interpretation des traditionellen Wohnbaues rund um einen Innenhof.

Edvard Ravnikar
Revolutionsplatz | Square of the Revolution
Ljubljana 1960–82

62

With the residential complex "Ferant-Garden" (1964–76) in the immediate vicinity, Ravnikar demonstrated the importance of the historic architecture of the turn of the century and the traditional open spaces in a residential district – with courtyard areas on the one side and streets on the other. He used the existing road network as a point of departure for the new buildings on the border (up to the lots adjacent to the road). In this way he created a contemporary interpretation of the traditional residential architecture surrounding a courtyard. As already mentioned, our modernism has not been determined by Ravnikar's work only. His influence can be found in the best works of his disciples, also in works achieved in our time. These works are not characterized by formal similarities – a justified objection to the Plečnik-school – they can much more be seen as the obvious expression of related views of architecture. Unlike the Plečnik-school which was founded mainly on the genius of its teacher, Ravnikar's school was system-oriented towards architectural research. It reflects his wide intellectual horizon, his interests not only in architecture itself, but also in global events, in art, philosophy, history, etc. Ravnikar's school was a peculiar laboratory of architecture, town planning and design pursuing many different tasks closely connected with current concerns. Experimenting with plasticity was crucial to the creative work. Yet still more emphatically than formal issues of architecture, Ravnikar taught discipline of thought, work approach and the method of architectural production.

Wie gesagt, wurde unser Modernismus nicht nur von Ravnikars Arbeiten geprägt. Sein Einfluss ist in den besten Arbeiten seiner Schüler zu finden, auch in Werken, die noch in unserer Zeit entstehen. Diese Arbeiten zeigen keine formalen Verwandtschaften – ein berechtigter Einwand gegen die Plečnik-Schule – sie sind eher ein offensichtlicher Ausdruck verwandter Architekturansichten und Orientierungsbemühungen. Im Gegensatz zur Plečnik-Schule, die vor allem auf dem Genius des Lehrers beruhte, war Ravnikars Schule systematisch und auf die Erforschung der Architektur ausgerichtet. In ihr spiegeln sich die Weite seines intellektuellen Horizonts, seine Interessen nicht nur für das Fach, sondern auch für das Geschehen in der Welt, für die Kunst, Philosophie, Geschichte usw. Ravnikars Schule war ein eigenartiges Laboratorium der Architektur, des Städtebaues und Designs, in dem an den verschiedensten, mit den Problemen der damaligen Zeit eng verbundenen Aufgaben gearbeitet wurde. In der schöpferischen Arbeit hatte das bildnerische Experiment die zentrale Rolle. Doch nachdrücklicher als die Architekturformen lehrte Ravnikar die Denkdisziplin, das Herangehen an die Arbeit und die Methode des architektonischen Schaffens.

Die Architektur der sogenannten „Ravnikar-Schule" zeichnet sich durch ein klares Architekturkonzept aus, das stets Reflex eines größeren Raumes ist, durch eine erfinderische und lesbare Formkonzeption, die auch dem bescheidensten Detail den gebührenden Platz zuweist, sowie durch eine kühn durchdachte, plastisch geformte Konstruktion, die den konzeptuellen Ausgangs-

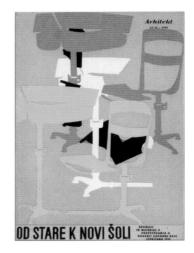

Zeitschrift Architekt Nr. 12-13, 1954
„Von der alten zu einer neuen Schule"
"From the old school to the new"
Cover Edvard Ravnikar

64

The architecture of the so-called "Ravnikar-school" is characterized by a clear architectural concept which always reflects a larger space, by an inventive and readable concept of form granting the simplest detail its due place as well as by a boldly conceived, three-dimensional structure determining the conceptual point of departure of the building both with regard to the organisation of inner space and of architectural expression. Already the works of the first generation of Ravnikar's diploma students reveal extraordinary technical and technological power of innovation. Inventiveness compensated the low level of development of the domestic construction industry.

The structural and constructional realism can maybe best be seen in the architecture of Savin Sever, particularly because of the formal strictness which is entirely subordinate to the logic of the building. His designs are classically symmetrical with typical correct geometry. This is the minimalism of exposed concrete, steel and glass (workshops of the Institute for partially deaf-mute people, 1962–63, centre of the Automobile Club, 1967–68, Mladinska knjiga Printing House, 1963–66, Merkur hardware store, 1968–70, two commercial towers and Astra department store, 1963–70, all in Ljubljana as well as the fair exposition building of the Gorenjski sejem in Kranj, 1970–71). A free organic arrangement of the building complex is characteristic of the work of Milan Mihelič (one department store in Osijek, 1963–67 and another in Novi Sad, 1968–72, international automatic telephone exchange, Ljubljana, 1972–78) and of Miloš Bonče (commercial building in the Šiška district in Ljubljana, 1960–64).

Stanko Kristl
Kindergarten Mladi rod
Ljubljana 1972

Savin Sever
Garagen im Montagebau | prefap garages
1964

punkt des Bauwerkes, sowohl im Sinne der Gliederung des Innenraumes als auch des architektonischen Ausdrucks bestimmt. Schon die Arbeiten der ersten Generation der Diplomanden Ravnikars zeigen eine außerordentliche technische und technologische Innovationskraft. Der Erfindungsgeist kompensierte den niedrigen Entwicklungsstand der einheimischen Bauindustrie.

Der Struktur- und Konstruktionsrealismus ist vielleicht am besten in der Architektur von Savin Sever sichtbar, gerade wegen der Formstrenge, die völlig der Logik des Baues untergeordnet ist. Seine Entwürfe sind klassisch symmetrisch, mit einer typischen richtigen Geometrie. Das ist der Minimalismus des Sichtbetons, des Stahls und Glases (Lehrwerkstätten der Anstalt für hörbehinderte Jugendliche, 1962–63, Zentrum des Automobilklubs, 1967–68, Druckerei des Verlages Mladinska knjiga, 1963–66, Warenhaus Merkur, 1968–70, zwei Hochhäuser und Warenhaus Astra, 1963–70, alle in Ljubljana, sowie das Ausstellungsgebäude des Gorenjski sejem in Kranj, 1970–71).

Eine freiere, organische Gliederung der Bauensembles ist typisch für das Werk von Milan Mihelič (je ein Warenhaus in Osijek, 1963–67 und Novi Sad, 1968–72, Internationale automatische Telefonzentrale, Ljubljana, 1972–78) sowie für Miloš Bonče (Geschäftshaus im Stadtteil Šiška in Ljubljana, 1960–64).

Die Bauten von Stanko Kristl (Wohnhäuser in Ljubljana, 1956–59, Geschäfts- und Wohnhausanlagen in Velenje, 1960–63 und Kranj, 1963–65, Kinderkrippe und Kindergarten Mladi rod,

65

Katalog | catalogue
„Die neue Architektur in Slowenien"
"The recent architecture in Slovenia"
Herausgeber | editor Stane Bernik
Ljubljana 1968

The buildings by Stanko Kristl (residential buildings in Ljubljana, 1956–59, commercial and residential buildings in Velenje, 1960–63 and Kranj, 1963–65, kindergarten Mladi rod, 1972, as well as diagnostic-therapeutic-service facility of the Clinical Centre in Ljubljana, 1968–77) are characterized by an extremely functional arrangement of spaces and a subtle composition of façades which is often referred to as "graphic art of the building shell".

Due to his extremely consequent layouts for apartments, Ilija Arnautović was able to achieve modern living standard in public housing. He researched the possibilities of industrialization and prefabrication in residential housing and proved that high-quality architecture is also possible with prefabricated construction.

It is understandably easier to recognize the dialogue between modern and traditional in buildings erected outside of the urban environment. We refer to our locally recognizable contribution to "regionalism" by the pioneer performance of Janez Lajovic (Hotel Prisank in Kranjska gora, 1961–62 and later Hotel Kanin in Bovec, 1969–73), the motel by Grega Košak (Motel Turist in Grosuplje, 1968–70), the elementary school by Majda Dobravec-Lajovic (Kranjska gora, 1965–70), and the particularly poetic architecture of Oton Jugovec (reconstruction of the church in Reteče 1970–74, roofing of the archaeological finds Gutenwerth, Otok pri Dravi, 1973, Baza 20 in Kočevski Rog, 1986–88, several detached houses, etc.).

1972, und einzelne Bauobjekte des Klinikzentrums in Ljubljana, 1968–77) sind gekennzeichnet durch eine äußerst funktionelle Raumgliederung und durch eine gestalterisch subtile Fassadenkomposition, die oft geradezu als „Graphik der Gebäudehülle" bezeichnet wurde. Ilija Arnautović erreichte mit äußerst konsequent durchdachten Wohnungsgrundrissen für einen modernen Standard im öffentlichen Wohnbau, erforschte die Möglichkeiten der Industrialisierung und Vorfertigung und bewies, dass es auch mit der Fertigbauweise möglich ist, qualitativ gute Architektur zu schaffen.

Der Dialog Moderne – Tradition ist verständlicherweise eher an Gebäuden außerhalb des städtischen Umfeldes erkennbar. Es geht um unseren, örtlich erkennbaren Beitrag zum „Regionalismus" mit der Pionierleistung von Janez Lajovic (Hotel Prisank, Kranjska gora, 1961–62, Hotel Kanin in Bovec, 1969–73), mit dem Motel von Grega Košak (Motel Turist, Grosuplje, 1968–70), der Volksschule von Majda Dobravec-Lajovic (Kranjska gora, 1965–70), und besonders poetisch mit der Architektur von Oton Jugovec (Wiederaufbau der Kirche in Reteče 1970–74, Überdachung der archäologischen Ausgrabungen Gutenwerth, Otok pri Dravi, 1973, Baza 20 in Kočevski Rog, 1986–88, mehrere Einfamilienhäuser u.a.).

Die zweite Generation der Diplomanden Ravnikars – nach erfolgreichen Wettbewerben mit Bauten auch in den anderen Teilrepubliken des damaligen Jugoslawien präsent – war sich bewusst, wie wichtig die Erhaltung der „Identität des Raumes, der Formen, der Tradition und des Temperaments"[5]

66

Janez Lajovic
Hotel Prisank
Kranjska gora 1961–62

The second generation of Ravnikar's diploma students were able to accomplish important buildings with award-winning projects also in other constituent republics of the former Yugoslavia and were equally aware of the importance of maintaining the "identity of space, forms, traditions and temperament"[5] to be seen most distinctly in the work of Marko Mušič (Memorial Hall in Kolašin, Montenegro,1969–75), but also in the work of the group Biro 71 (Štefan Kacin, Jurij Princes, Bogdan Spindler and Marjan Uršič – Cultural Centre Skopje, Macedonia,1969–81).

Slovenian architecture is a very heterogeneous mosaic of a great variety of works which is understandable given the geographic, cultural and climatic differences of the country. Therefore the question arises whether the syntagm "Slovenian architecture" expresses more than "works of Slovenian architects" or "architecture in the territory of Slovenia." It is a strange paradox that in this sense especially the architecture of the Ravnikar-school is an exception, although it is clearly recognizable that it is responsive to the particularities of the environment. In the Karst differently than in coastal areas and in Kranj differently than in Koper. But in spite of all the different personal views of the numerous architects it is obvious that their works are the result of related creative approaches.

ist, am deutlichsten kommt dies in der Arbeit von Marko Mušič zum Ausdruck (Gedenkstätte in Kolašin, Montenegro, 1969–75), aber auch bei der Gruppe Biro 71 (Štefan Kacin, Jurij Princes, Bogdan Spindler und Marjan Uršič – Kulturzentrum Skopje, Mazedonien, 1969–81).

Die slowenische Architektur ist ein sehr heterogenes Mosaik unterschiedlichster Werke, was angesichts der geographischen, kulturellen und klimatischen Vielfalt des Landes verständlich ist. Daher ergibt sich die Frage, ob das Syntagma „slowenische Architektur" mehr ausdrückt als die Tatsache, dass es um Werke slowenischer Architekten oder um Architektur im slowenischen Raum geht. Ein eigenartiges Paradoxon ist es, dass in diesem Sinne gerade die Architektur der Ravnikar-Schule eine Ausnahme darstellt, obwohl sie auf die Besonderheiten des Umfeldes deutlich erkennbar reagiert, im Karst anders als im Küstenland und in Kranj anders als in Koper. Doch trotz aller Verschiedenheit der persönlichen Sichtweisen der zahlreichen Architekten ist es offensichtlich, dass ihre Arbeiten als Ergebnis verwandter schöpferischer Ausgangspunkte entstanden sind. Es stellt sich die Frage, ob die slowenische Architektur am Beginn des dritten Jahrtausends noch irgendetwas an unseren Raum bindet. Daher wäre es notwendig, nochmals auf Ravnikar zu hören: „Die Welt, in der wir leben, muss und wird immer zwei Erscheinungsformen haben: eine vergängliche, zeitliche und eine verhältnismäßig dauerhafte, zeitlose. Daher wollen wir unsere Siedlungen, Städte und Landschaften nicht als unberührbare Denkmäler betrachten, aber auch nicht als eingeebneten Boden, auf dem wir irgendetwas Beliebiges errichten können."[6]

5 Marko Mušič, Kolašin, katalog razstave (Kolašin, Ausstellungskatalog), Društvo oblikovalcev Slovenije v sodelovanju z Moderno galerijo, Ljubljana 1977, Seite 3
6 Edo Ravnikar, Sedem naglavnih grehov (Die sieben Hauptsünden ...) Seite 924-925

5 Marko Mušič, Kolašin, katalog razstave (Kolašin, exhibition catalogue), Društvo oblikovalcev Slovenije v sodelovanju z Moderno galerijo, Ljubljana 1977, page 3
6 Edo Ravnikar, Sedem naglavnih grehov (The seven deadly sins ...) page 924–925

67

The question arises whether Slovenian architecture in the beginning of the third millennium is still in any way bound to our geographic area. Therefore it would be necessary once again to listen to what Ravnikar has to say: "The world we live in must and will always have two manifestations: a transitory, temporal one and a relatively permanent, timeless one. Therefore we do not want to consider our settlements, cities and landscapes as untouchable monuments, but also not as levelled ground on which we can erect anything we want."[6]

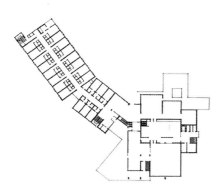

Branko Simčič, Milan Mihelič, Ilija Arnautović
Ausstellungsgelände Halle A | Commercial Exhibition Grounds, Ljubljana
Branko Simčič, Hall A, 1954–58
Marko Šlajmer, Pavillon E, 1960
Milan Mihelič, Hall C, 1965–67

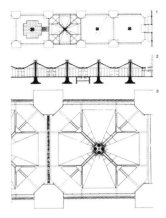

68

Edo Mihevc
Impex Gebäude | Impex Building
Ljubljana 1953–57

Emil Medvešček, Oton Jugovec
Hauptsitz der Gewerkschaft
Headquarters of the Main Cooperative Association
Ljubljana 1953–55

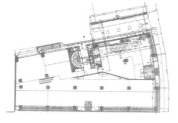

Edvard Ravnikar
Filiale der slowenischen Nationalbank
Branch of the National Bank of Slovenia
Kranj 1959–62

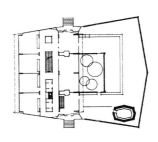

Miloš Bonča
Geschäftsgebäude in Šiška
Commercial Building in Šiška
Ljubljana 1960–64

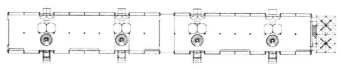

Savin Sever
Kaufhaus Merkur
Merkur Department Store
Ljubljana 1968–70

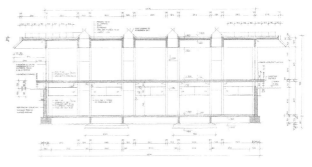

Savin Sever
Astra und Geschäftstürme | Astra and Commerce Towers
Ljubljana 1963–70

Milan Mihelič
Turm S2 und MATC-Gebäude
Tower S2 and MATC Building
Ljubljana 1972–78

Edvard Ravnikar
Hotel Creina
Kranj 1968–70

Edo Mihevc
„Kozolec" Wohnanlage | residential building
Ljubljana 1953–57

Stanko Kristl
Wohn- und Geschäftsgebäude | residential and commercial building
Velenje 1960–63

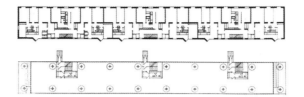

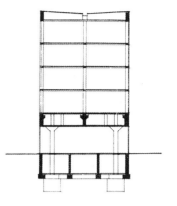

Stanko Kristl
Kindergarten Mladi rod
Ljubljana 1972

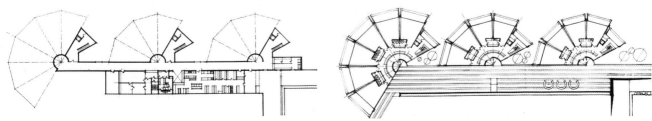

Danilo Furst
Volksschule | primary school
Stražišče pri Kranju 1954–59

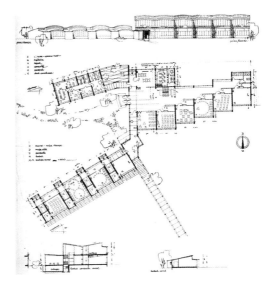

80

Milan Mihelič
Kaufhaus | department store
Osijek, Kroatien | Croatia 1963–67

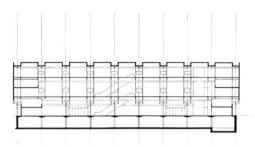

Milan Mihelič
Kaufhaus Stoteks | Stoteks Department Store
Novi Sad, Serbien | Serbia 1968–72

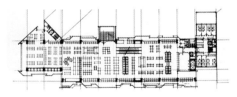

Savin Sever
Druckerei und Verlag Mladinska knjiga
Mladinska knjiga Printing and Edition House
Ljubljana 1966

Savin Sever
Technikzentrum AMZS
Technical Center AMZS
Ljubljana 1967–68

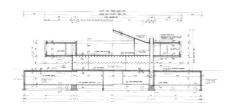

Oton Jugovec
Kernreaktor des Jozef Štefan Instituts
Nuclear reactor of the Jozef Štefan Institute
Podgorica 1960–66

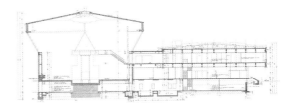

Oton Jugovec
„Baza 20"
Kočevski Rog 1986–88

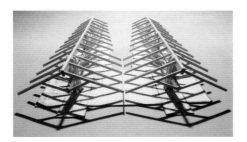

Milan Mihelič
Wohnhaus | apartment building
Ljubljana 1969–71

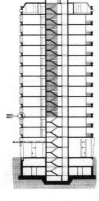

Oton Jugovec
Villa Repotočnik
Ljubljana 1969–78

Richard Vakaj
Villa Koler
Sp. Ščavnica (Unterstainz) 1976

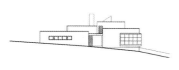

DIE SLOWENISCHE ARCHITEKTUR 1945-1980

Edvard Ravnikar
Wohn- und Geschäftsgebäude „Ferant-Garten"
Ferant Garden Residential and Business Complex
Ljubljana 1964–73

Edvard Ravnikar
Wohn- und Geschäftsgebäude
„Ferant-Garten"
Ferant Garden Residential
and Business Complex
Ljubljana 1964–73

ÜBER EIN ZITAT VON EDVARD RAVNIKAR:

„Architektur gibt es nur mehr in unterentwickelten Ländern"

"Only in underdeveloped countries can architecture still be found"

FRIEDRICH ACHLEITNER

Vortrag | lecture
Ravnikar-Symposium
3.12.2007

Ich weiß, man ist gut beraten, wenn man die oft provokanten, ironischen Aussprüche Edvard Ravnikars nicht auf die Goldwaage legt, aber man darf sie ebenso wenig unterschätzen. Je versteckter die Wahrheit ist, umso hartnäckiger behauptet sie sich. Und ich bringe den Satz *Architektur gibt es nur mehr in unterentwickelten Ländern*, den ich vermutlich vor rund vierzig Jahren von ihm gehört habe, nicht aus dem Kopf.

Damals, Ende der 1960er Jahre, ich darf das in Erinnerung rufen, hat man an den Architekturschulen in technologischen Utopien geschwelgt. Alles war beweglich, flexibel und variabel, hat sich an den jüngsten Entwicklungen orientiert, das Auto war schon lange nicht mehr das Vorbild einer funktionalen oder gar funktionalistischen Architektur, sondern die Raumkapsel. Es ist schon möglich, dass damals in Ländern, die sich noch nicht an diesem Wettrennen beteiligen konnten, der resignative Eindruck entstand, dass Architektur, der Schwerkraft ausgeliefert, mit Orten verbunden und in politische und kulturelle Zwangsjacken gesteckt, nur mehr in „unterentwickelten Ländern" eine Überlebenschance hatte. Damals behauptete etwa ein Buckminster Fuller bei einem Vortrag in Wien tatsächlich, der Wiener Stephansdom sei viel zu schwer, und man konnte daraus schließen, dass er damit meinte, dass er auch schlechte Architektur sei.

I know that you are well-advised not to weigh every word of Edvard Ravnikar's often provoking ironic remarks, but they are not to be underestimated either. The more the truth is hidden, the more persistently it stands its ground. And I cannot get the phrase I heard from him probably about forty years ago out of my head: *"Only in underdeveloped countries can architecture still be found"*.

At that time, at the end of the 1960s, if I may recall, schools of architecture revelled in technological utopias. Everything was mobile, flexible and variable, geared to the latest developments, for a long time already the car had ceased to be the example of functional let alone functionalistic architecture; it had been replaced by the space capsule.
It may very well be that in countries that in those days were not yet able to take part in this race, you might have had the resigned impression that architecture, subjected to the forces of gravity, linked to specific places and tied up in political and cultural straitjackets, could only survive in "underdeveloped countries". At that time, for example, Buckminster Fuller actually declared, in a lecture in Vienna, that Vienna's St. Stephen's Cathedral was much too heavy, from which one might conclude that he meant that it was also poor architecture.

Leider kann ich mich nicht mehr an den Ton erinnern, in dem Ravnikar diesen Satz sagte. Es war sicher ein Unterton dabei, der dem „alten Fuchs" entsprach, der damals rund zwanzig Jahre jünger war, als meine Generation es heute ist. Ich muss noch einschränken, dass ich Edvard Ravnikar nicht wirklich gut kannte, ja dass ich eigentlich nur eine, allerdings dreitägige Begegnung mit ihm hatte, bei der er uns (meine Frau Barbara und mich) im Jahre 1971 durch Ljubljana führte. Unsere Ziele waren fast ausschließlich Bauten von Josef Plečnik, seine Wohnanlage Ferantsgarten, gerade im Fertigwerden, streiften wir im Vorbeigehen, und vom Hotel in Kranj gab er mir etwas Material mit, weil ich darüber schreiben wollte. Für die Fahrt nach Kärnten empfahl er uns einige gute Wirtshäuser und wir bekamen einen Einführungsvortrag über den „Cviček". In Erinnerung ist mir eine weitere Bemerkung, die mir seine Persönlichkeit zu charakterisieren schien: Als er am zweiten Tag zu unserer Verabredung beträchtlich zu spät kam, entschuldigte er sich damit, dass er einen Termin in der Klinik hatte, und da er die Privilegien eines Professors nicht in Anspruch nehmen wollte, er eben mit allen anderen Patienten lange warten musste. Ich dachte mir damals, diese Geschichte müsste man den Wiener Professoren erzählen.

Unfortunately I cannot remember the tone in which Ravnikar said this. Without doubt there was an undertone typical for that "old fox", who at the time was approximately twenty years younger than my generation is today. I should qualify that by saying that I did not really know Edvard Ravnikar very well, that in fact I actually only met him once, but that was for three whole days, when he showed us (my wife and me) Ljubljana in 1971. Our targets almost exclusively concentrated on Josef Plečnik, his housing estate "Ferant Garden" which at that time was about to be completed, we visited in passing and he gave me some material on the hotel in Kranj because I wanted to write about it. For the trip to Carinthia he recommended some good pubs and gave us an introductory lecture on the "Cviček". I remember another remark which I thought was characteristic for his personality. When he was considerably late for our second meeting, he apologized by saying that he had an appointment at the hospital and since he did not make use of the privileges of a professor, he had to wait for a long time with all the other patients. It occurred to me, that this story would have to be told to Viennese professors.

Nun zum Thema:

Schon allein die Bezeichnung „unterentwickeltes Land" – wenn er damit das damalige Jugoslawien meinte – war eine Koketterie. Er wusste genau, dass wir österreichischen Studenten und jungen Architekten in den 1950er und 1960er Jahren teilweise neidisch nach Jugoslawien blickten, denn dort erschien uns die architektonische Szene vitaler und bunter, vor allem was Slowenien und Kroatien betraf. Hier hatte nicht zuletzt, nach dem monarchistischen Mitteleuropa und dem Mythos der Otto-Wagner-Schule, der Einfluss Le Corbusiers fruchtbringend gewirkt.

Wir hatten, wenn ich das gestehen darf, die damalige zeitgenössische jugoslawische Architektur eher zufällig entdeckt, und zwar über den Umweg der anonymen Architektur, die damals für uns bis hinunter nach Griechenland und in die Türkei ein Forschungsgegenstand besonderer Art war. Uns trieb nicht so sehr ein historisches Interesse, sondern eine Quellensuche für die Entwicklung neuer Wohnformen, vor allem im Siedlungsbau. Meine erste Reise um 1960 mit dem Zelt von Istrien bis hinunter zum Neretva-Delta und über Sarajewo zurück (wo man noch zwischen Bogumilengräbern die Zelte aufschlagen konnte) eröffnete für mich eine neue Welt, nicht nur in architektonischer Hinsicht. Und auf den späteren Reisen stand man immer wieder überraschend vor Bauten, die wie „vom Himmel gefallen" wirkten, die bereits eine Zukunft einlösten, von der wir nur träumen konnten.

Now to the subject-matter:

Just the designation "underdeveloped country" – if he meant the Yugoslavia of that period – was coquetry. He knew perfectly well that we Austrian students and young architects in the 1950s and 1960s were looking partly with envy in the direction of Yugoslavia, because the architectural scene there seemed to us to be more vivid and varied, particularly with regard to Slovenia and Croatia, where after monarchist central European tradition and the myth of the Otto-Wagner-School, also the influence of Le Corbusier was fruitful.

We had, if I may confess, discovered contemporary Yugoslav architecture rather by chance and did so by means of the detour of anonymous architecture which then was a special object of research way down to Greece and into Turkey. We were driven not so much by historical interest, but rather by the search for sources for the development of new forms of residential buildings, particularly in housing projects. My first trip, around 1960, with a tent from Istria down to the Neretva Delta and back via Sarajevo (where you could still pitch your tent amidst Bogumil tombs) opened up a new world for me, not only with regard to architecture. And during later trips one was time and again taken by surprise when one found oneself standing in front of buildings which looked like they had "fallen from heaven", which already redeemed a future we could only dream of.

Mit der Aufarbeitung der Wiener Moderne, der Otto Wagner-Schule (zunächst angeregt in den 1950er Jahren von dem zehn Jahre älteren Studienkollegen Johannes Spalt) kamen auch Max Fabiani und Josef Plečnik in unser Blickfeld. Ich mache jetzt einen größeren Zeitsprung zu Edvard Ravnikar. Erlauben Sie mir, um ihnen noch kurz einen Einblick in die Situation um 1970 zu geben, dass ich zwei Absätze aus meiner ersten Beschäftigung mit einem Bau von ihm vorlese:

Zitat: *Architektur und Urbanismus (bauforum 24/1971)*
        Wohnanlage „Ferantsgarten", 1964–71

In Ljubljana steht man unserer „neueren Entdeckung", dass bauliche Objekte nicht als isolierte Organismen, sondern in einem größeren städtebaulichen Zusammenhang zu sehen sind, etwas lächelnd gegenüber. In der Stadt hat es die Trennung von Architektur und Städtebau nie gegeben. Jedenfalls ist die Tradition des urbanen Denkens seit Camillo Sitte, Max Fabiani und Josef Plečnik ungebrochen. Und auch die gegenwärtige Architektur ist von dieser Tradition des Denkens bestimmt. Das macht die bauliche Faszination dieser Stadt aus, in der man auf Schritt und Tritt die Auseinandersetzungen spürt, die von verschiedenen Architekten mit dieser Stadt geführt wurden.

94

In the course of reviewing Viennese modernity and the Otto-Wagner-School, (initially inspired in the 1950s by my fellow student Johannes Spalt, 10 years my senior) we also came to focus on Max Fabiani and Josef Plečnik also increasingly. And now would like to make a leap forward in time to Edvard Ravnikar. In order to give you a brief impression of the situation around 1970, allow me to read you two paragraphs of my first papers on one of his buildings

Quote: *Architecture and urbanism (bauforum 24/1971)*
        Housing estate „Ferant Garden", 1964–71

In Ljubljana, our "new discovery" that built objects should not be considered as isolated organisms, but as integrated in a bigger urban planning context, is smiled at a little bit condescendingly. In this city architecture and town planning were never separated. The tradition of urbane thinking has in any case never been interrupted since Camillo Sitte, Max Fabiani and Josef Plečnik. And also present-day architecture is determined by this tradition of thinking. This makes this city's architecture so fascinating and at every turn you sense various architects' confrontation with it.

Vielleicht gehört es auch zur Tradition der slowenischen Republik- und Nationalhauptstadt mit rund 200.000 Einwohnern, dass in ihr jeweils eine Architekturanschauung dominierte, sei sie in einer Person oder in einer Schule verkörpert. Das Erbe Josef Plečniks, der wie kein anderer diese Stadt prägte, wurde zweifellos von Edvard Ravnikar übernommen. Er übernahm aber auch ein typisch slowenisches Geschick, in den grobmaschigen Registraturen der modernen Architekturgeschichtsschreibung nicht aufzuscheinen. Es scheint, als stellte sich hier ein Minderheitenproblem ganz besonderer Natur zur Diskussion. Die großen Nationalstaaten haben eben mehr und bessere Gelegenheiten, ihre kulturellen Produktionen in das Licht der Weltöffentlichkeit zu stellen. Erst in Laibach versteht man Ravnikars Anschauung, dass Architektur etwas Lokales ist und nur aus dessen Verhältnissen zu verstehen sei.

Man könnte zuerst die Frage stellen, war die Situation, in der Edvard Ravnikar arbeitete, wirklich eine „unterentwickelte" und hinkten seine Antworten, die er auf die Probleme seiner Stadt und seiner Zeit fand, wirklich hinter der Zeit nach? Schon hier blitzt die Fragwürdigkeit einer modernistischen Fortschrittsskala auf, und man könnte behaupten, wer die Architektur nicht aus ihrer historischen und gesellschaftlichen Verantwortung entlässt, muss zu den Trends seiner Zeit zumindest eine kritische Distanz bewahren.

95

Maybe it is also part of the tradition of the Slovenian Republic and the nation's capital city with its approximately 200 000 inhabitants that one architectural approach at a time was dominant, embodied in one person or school. The heritage of Josef Plečnik who left his mark on this city like no other, was doubtlessly taken up by Edvard Ravnikar. But he also had to accept the typically Slovenian fate not to be mentioned in the wide-meshed registries of modern architecture historiography. A very special kind of minority problem seems to be at stake here. The big nation states simply have more and better opportunities to present their cultural productions in the light of the world public. It is only in Ljubljana that one understands Ravnikar's concept of architecture as something local which can only be understood considering its circumstances.

The first question would be whether the situation in which Edvard Ravnikar worked really was "underdeveloped" and whether the answers he found to the problems of his city and his time were really behind the times? Already at this point the precariousness of a modernistic scale of progress flashes through one's mind and one might say that whoever does not release architecture from its historical and social responsibility must at least keep a critical distance to the trends of his time.

Sie merken schon, Ravnikars provokante Aussage führt uns unvermeidbar in das Spannungsfeld lokaler und globaler Architekturen, und ich möchte nicht die eine gegen die andere ausspielen, sondern versuchen, zu beiden eine halbwegs erträgliche Distanz zu halten. Ich bewege mich hier, selbstverständlich, im Bereich von Vermutungen und Behauptungen. Ich möchte auch nicht einen Antagonismus zwischen internationaler, globaler und regionaler, bzw. lokaler Architektur konstruieren, was ohnehin nur ein fragwürdiges Konstrukt wäre, eher noch zwischen zwei Arbeitsfeldern und Zweckhaltungen, die sich in der Gegenwart durch die Entwicklung oder Explosion der Informationsmedien in einer besonderen Weise artikulieren. Es gab in der Architektur immer schon überregionale Phänomene, wenn sie auch nicht den ganzen Globus betrafen. So war die Gotik durch die Wanderungen der Bauhütten (etwa von Paris bis Budapest) eine expansive, nicht an Orte gebundene Architektur, die natürlich von den örtlichen personellen und materialen Ressourcen abhängig war. Der Barock, als expansive „Propagandaarchitektur" des Christentums, schaffte es sogar bis Südamerika. Architekten wie Giovanni Lorenzo Bernini (1598–1680), der auch in Paris mit großen Ehren empfangen wurde, könnte man bereits als „Stararchitekten" ihrer Zeit bezeichnen. Und man darf nicht vergessen, es handelte sich um „Oberschichtphänomene", um Machtdemonstrationen teilweise verwandter und europäisch vernetzter Herrscherfamilien, und um ein sehr kleines Segment der architektonischen Produktion, eben vorwiegend um Kirchen, Klöster und Schlösser.

96

As you can see, Ravnikar's provocative statement inevitably puts us in the field of tension between local and global architecture and I do not want to play one off against the other, but want to try to keep a somewhat tolerable distance to both. Of course, I am obviously relying on speculation and allegations in this matter. I do not want to construct antagonism between international, global and regional or local architecture either, which in any case would only be a dubious creation, but rather between two fields of work and purpose-oriented attitudes articulated at present particularly through the development or the explosion of information media. In architecture there have always been supraregional phenomena, even if they did not affect the entire globe. Gothic architecture, for example, due to the migration of the guilds of masons (e.g., from Paris to Budapest), was expansive and not tied to particular places and obviously had to rely on the local resources concerning material and personnel. Baroque, the expansive "propaganda architecture" of Christianity even made it to South America. Architects such as Giovanni Lorenzo Bernini (1598–1680) who was also welcomed in Paris with great honours, could already be designated as star architects of their day. And one must not forget that these were "upper class phenomena", demonstrations of power of sometimes related dynasties which were part of European networks and that they represented a very small segment of the architectural production, for the most part churches, monasteries and castles.

Ich möchte, um vielleicht im Thema weiter und Edvard Ravnikar näher zu kommen, einen Gegensatz konstruieren, ein Spannungsfeld, dem heute die Architekten besonders ausgesetzt sind und das in irgend einer Form auch immer vorhanden war, aber durch die Schnelligkeit der Informationsnetze eine besondere Qualität entwickelte.

Nennen wir sie beim Namen: Die sogenannten Stararchitekten, ich möchte sie lieber Großarchitekten nennen, die internationalen, ja globalen Opinionleader, sind eine Kaste von individualistischen Trend-, Themen-, Bild- und Formproduzenten, die zu Recht oder zu Unrecht, den Fortschritt für sich in Anspruch nehmen und (oft schnell wechselnde) Kataloge mit Tendenzen anbieten. Wir lebten nicht im Zeitalter des Neoliberalismus, wenn damit nicht auch Marktgesetze, Moden, Konkurrenzen oder Spiele öffentlicher Präsenz instrumentalisiert werden würden. Ich möchte versuchen, darüber wertfrei zu sprechen, auch wenn diese Vokabel einmal in Verruf geraten ist. Man kann ja nicht leugnen, dass ein Frank Gehry, eine Zaha Hadid, ein Rem Koolhaas oder (anders herum) auch ein Peter Zumthor in den Gehirnen von tausenden Architekten nicht etwas bewegt hätten. Nicht nur in den Gehirnen von Architekten. Der sogenannte Bilbao-Effekt ist ja kein Hirngespinst, sondern eine reale Veränderung des Lebens einer Stadt. Und nach Vals pilgern nicht nur Architekten, nur wissen viele Kulturmenschen nicht, dass sie dort auch Plečnik begegnen.

In order to maybe continue with our subject and get a closer look at Edvard Ravnikar, I would like to point out a contradiction, a field of tension to which architects today are particularly exposed and which in some way always existed, but which has, due to the velocity of the information networks, developed a special quality.

Let's call them by their name: the so-called star architects, I prefer to call them big architects, the international, even global opinion leaders, are a caste of individual producers of trends, subjects, images and forms who rightly or wrongly lay claim to progress and offer (often rapidly changing) catalogues with tendencies. We would not be living in the age of neoliberalism, if this would not involve an instrumentalization of market laws, fashions, competitions or games of public presence. I will try to talk about this in a value-free way, even if this expression once fell into disrepute. It cannot be denied that a Frank Gehry, a Zaha Hadid, a Rem Kolhaas or (the other way round) also a Peter Zumthor did very well move something in the brains of thousands of architects. Not only in the brains of architects. The so-called Bilbao-effect is no delusion, but a real change in the life of a city. And not only architects make pilgrimages to Vals, only many civilized persons do not know that they also meet Plečnik there.

Das Problem der Großarchitekturen ist auch weniger das inhaltliche Angebot (die Absicht, die oft verstimmen könnte) als das Thema der globalen Distribution von Effekten, Neuigkeiten, Sensationen. In dieser Welt des Bauens werden ja Mechanismen bedient, die sich von den Niederungen des Tourismus bis zu Städte- oder Konzernkonkurrenzen aufschwingen. Und paradoxer Weise werden nicht nur Standorte aufgewertet, ins Licht gestellt, sondern auch neu erfunden oder erfolgreich ins Bild gesetzt.

Man kann behaupten, das Segment der „Großarchitektur" ist nicht nur größer geworden, sondern es hat auch vielfach ein Rollenwechsel stattgefunden: Museen, Ausstellungshallen, Opern- und Konzerthäuser, Zentralen von Weltfirmen und Konzernen, etc. etc, müssen eine weltweite visuelle Konkurrenz bestehen, wenn sie überhaupt wahrgenommen werden wollen. Hier vereinigt sich die neoliberale Wirtschaft mit einem individualistischen Ranking, die Spielflächen heben sich zunehmend von ihren Lebensräumen ab, die Architektur geht an die Börsen und unterwirft sich den Interessen von Managern und Aktionären. Damit verbunden sind die Begriffe von Geschwindigkeit und Abschreibbarkeit. Diese Architektur wird für den schnellen Markt geplant, die Abschreibefrist dauert höchstens dreißig Jahre, dann kommt die Architektur auf den Müll, wenn sie nicht schon lange vorher formal verschlissen wurde. Bauten degenerieren zu merkbaren Symbolen des Wandels, ihr Überleben ist die Dokumentation,

98

The problem of big architecture indeed is less the content offered (the intent that could often annoy) than rather the subject of global distribution of effects, news, sensations. In this world of building, mechanisms come into play which rise from the lowlands of tourism to the competitions between cities and groups of companies. And paradoxically locations are not only upgraded, highlighted, but also reinvented or are successfully set up.

One can say that the segment of "big architecture" has not only grown, but that often also roles were changed: museums, exhibition halls, operas and concert halls, headquarters of international companies and concerns, etc,, etc. have to face world-wide visual competition, if they want to be noticed at all. Here neoliberal economy is combined with individualist ranking, the playing-fields increasingly contrast with their living space, architecture enters the stock exchange and submits to the interests of managers and shareholders. This is linked to the concepts of speed and tax deductability. This architecture is designed for a rapid market, the depreciation period amounts to 30 years at most, then the architecture is thrown out, if it has not been formally worn out a long time before. Buildings degenerate to become clearly noticeable symbols of this change: they survive in documentation, not through conservation.

nicht ihre Erhaltung. Natürlich hängt diese Architektur auch mit dem Wandel der technischen Bauproduktion zusammen, ihre Wiege lag vielleicht in den großen Weltausstellungen des 19. Jahrhunderts, der Kristallpalast ist noch immer das „Flaggschiff" eines Mythos der revolutionär fortschreitenden Moderne. Selbstverständlich fordert diese „Großarchitektur" zu höchsten individuellen Leistungen heraus, die als Maßstäbe wieder an die stillen Orte des lokalen Bauens zurückkehren. Und ich weiß, dass man diese eine Seite des Bauens nicht isoliert betrachten kann. Sie verändert zu sehr unser Leben und wir sind auch, ehrlich gestanden, viel zu abhängig von ihr. Wie sieht aber die andere Seite aus, die von der Moderne als konservativ, wenn nicht reaktionär denunziert wurde? Wie sieht dagegen ein Architekturbegriff eines Josef Plečnik aus, der nicht imstande war (besser: nicht wollte), die Architektur von den einfachen aber umfangreichen Grundlagen ihrer Existenz abzukoppeln.

Eine Architektur, die sich auf den Menschen, auf seine soziale Befindlichkeit, sein Denken, seine Geschichte, seine materiellen Bedürfnisse einlässt, kann seinen Lebensraum, seine Orte, seine Sozio- und Biotope nicht ignorieren. Die globale Schnelligkeit verwandelt sich automatisch in eine lokale Langsamkeit. Es ist ja nicht so, dass diese Lebenswelt (diese „kleine Welt" mit ihren Kleinarchitekten, die oft Großes leisten) nicht die große wahrnimmt. Aber sie reagiert anders, vielleicht behäbiger, vorsichtiger, skeptischer. Ich vermute, Edvard Ravnikar hat sich

Of course, this architecture also has to be seen in connection with the change in the technical production of buildings, its birth can maybe be dated in the great world fairs of the 19th century, the Crystal Palace still is the "flagship" of a myth of the revolutionary progress of modernity. This "big architecture" of course provokes highest individual performances which then return as standards to the quiet places of local building. And I know that this one side of building cannot be seen in an isolated way. It changes our life too much and we are, honestly speaking, also much too dependent on it. But what does the other side look like, the side which modernity denounces as conservative, if not reactionary? What, by contrast, is the concept of architecture of somebody like Josef Plečnik who could not (better: did not want to) disconnect architecture from the simple but extensive foundations of its existence.

Architecture that deals with people in their social situation, their thinking, their history, their material needs, cannot ignore their living space, their places, their sociotopes and biotopes. Global speed is automatically transformed into local slowness. As a matter of fact, this life-world (this "small world" with its small architects who often achieve great things) does indeed take notice of the big one. But it reacts differently, maybe more sedately, with more precaution, more scepticism. I suppose Edvard Ravnikar felt an obligation towards this world, although, as his town planning and big projects show, he had the makings of a "big architect". This was no comfortable but a radical position, and, metaphorically speaking, came close to the "priestly

dieser Welt verpflichtet gefühlt, obwohl er, das beweisen seine städtebaulichen Planungen und Großprojekte, das Zeug für einen „Großarchitekten" hatte. Das war keine bequeme, sondern eine radikale Position, das ist, im übertragenen Sinn, eine Annäherung an die „priesterliche Haltung", die sein Lehrer Plečnik gegenüber der Architektur eingefordert hat. Architektur, die in einem verbindlichen Lebensraum arbeitet, auf einer Baustelle, die der Architekt nicht nach Fertigstellung mit dem Privatjet verlässt, der ihr verantwortlich bleibt, hat andere Kriterien, und ich vermute, dass diese eher mit Beharrlichkeit, Nachhaltigkeit (um ein aus der Mode gekommenes Modewort zu verwenden), mit Dauerhaftigkeit, Beständigkeit bezeichnet werden können. Natürlich liegt es auf der Hand, dass solche Haltungen leicht als rückschrittlich und unterentwickelt denunziert werden können. Aber ich habe den Eindruck, dass Bauten, die mit einem größeren Zeithorizont entworfen werden, die das kollektive Gedächtnis akzeptieren, die eine kulturelle Erinnerung bewahren, dass solche Bauten nicht nur materiell weniger schnell altern, sondern auch in ihrer Wirkung jung bleiben. Um noch einmal den architektonischen Landesheiligen Josef Plečnik zu bemühen, ich habe noch bei jedem Besuch seiner Bauten Neues, Überraschendes entdeckt, immer wieder einen Gedanken mitgenommen, und wenn es nur ein kleiner, neuer Aspekt etwa in seiner Auseinandersetzung mit Gottfried Semper war.

100

attitude" his teacher Plečnik demanded with regard to architecture. Architecture intervening in a living space with responsibility, on a building site which the architect does not abandon in his or her private jet after completion, but for which he or she continues to assume responsibility, follows different criteria and I suppose that these will rather be called perseverance, sustainability (to use a word that once was 'in'), durability, permanence. It is easy of course to discard these attitudes as reactionary and underdeveloped. But I have the impression that buildings designed with a longer time horizon, that accept collective memory, that conserve a cultural remembrance, that such buildings not only age materially less quickly, but also their effect remains youthful. To refer once again to the architectural national patron saint, Josef Plečnik during each visit to his buildings I discovered something new, surprising, always came away with a new idea, be it only a small new aspect, for example, in his confrontation with Gottfried Semper.

Beispiel: Dialektik zwischen Struktur, Körperhaftigkeit, Raum und Fläche, Ornament. Fenster der Krypta der Herz-Jesu-Kirche in Prag (1928–31), aufgenommen vor drei Wochen. Die Krypta ist ein tonnengewölbter Raum mit einer kräftigen Ziegelstruktur. Bei den Fenstern, also dort wo diese durchbrochen wird, verwandelt sie sich in eine Fläche, ja eine Tapete, und die weiße Fläche, Prototyp für eine entmaterialisierte Oberfläche, kippt in ihr Gegenteil und bildet plötzlich ein starkes Volumen. So spricht Architektur mit ihren autonomen Mitteln.

Ich vermute, dass der 1970 gar nicht so „alte Fuchs" Edvard Ravnikar „unterentwickelt" als Metapher für etwas sehr Positives gebraucht hat, für etwas immer wieder Fortschrittliches weil Herausforderndes, nämlich für eine Architektur, die sich nicht nur von politischen, ökonomischen oder kommerziellen Interessen fesseln lässt, sondern bewusst ihre Verantwortung für alle Menschen und Lebensformen übernimmt, also über eine ästhetische Vermarktung hinaus auch ethische Kategorien akzeptiert. In Edvard Ravnikars Werk ist dieses Bemühen in allen seinen Arbeiten präsent, wenn er sich auch nicht der sogenannten „großen Welt" verschlossen hat. Vielleicht sollte man seine urbanistischen Planungen oder auch den ehemaligen „Platz der Revolution" einmal unter diesem Gesichtswinkel eines umfassenden Architekturbegriffs betrachten. Wenn sein Lehrer Plečnik in einer scheinbar alten Sprache neue Gedanken formulierte, und aus der intimen Kenntnis etwa der römischen Antike Anregungen zu neuen

Example: dialectics between structure, corporeality, space and surface, ornament. Windows of the crypt of the Church of the Sacred Heart in Prague (1928–31), photographed three weeks ago. The crypt is a room with a barrel vault and prominent brickwork. At the windows, i.e., where it is broken up, it becomes flat, one might even say it has the effect of a wallpapered surface, and the white surface, prototype of a dematerialised surface, is transformed into its opposite and all of a sudden creates a strong volume. In this way architecture speaks through its autonomous means.

I suppose that in 1970, Edvard Ravnikar, who at that time was not even so much of an "old fox", used "underdeveloped" as a metaphor for something very positive, for something that was always progressive, because it was challenging, i.e., because it was architecture that does not let itself become enchained by political, economic or commercial interests alone, but consciously assumes responsibility for all people and forms of living, i.e., accepts also ethic categories beyond aesthetic exploitation. In Edvard Ravnikars work, this effort can be felt throughout, even if he did not reject the call of the "great wide world". Maybe his urban planning or also the "Square of the Revolution" should once be discussed from this perspective of a comprehensive notion of architecture. While his teacher Plečnik formulated new ideas in seemingly old-fashioned language and gained inspiration for new daring spatial and formal concepts from an intimate knowledge e.g. of Roman antiquity, Ravnikar, in his reformulation of

kühnen Raum- und Formkonzepten holte, so hat Ravnikar in der Neuformulierung von Orten (etwa der platzartigen Erweiterung der Altstadt von Kranj) mit einer größeren Nähe zur Gegenwart und einem erweiterten Blickfeld Ähnliches mit dem sogenannten Genius Loci gemacht, indem er alles Vorgefundene und das Hinzugefügte zu einer neuen Einheit verband.

Und in diesem Sinne findet vielleicht Architektur wirklich nur mehr an „unterentwickelten Orten" statt (ich lasse absichtlich die Länder aus dem Spiel), oder besser, in kulturellen Situationen, die sich den Luxus der Langsamkeit, der Beständigkeit, der Verantwortlichkeit für den Menschen, des historischen Bewusstseins, der kollektiven Erinnerung und einer permanenten Reflexion des eigenen Standortes leisten können. Dazu braucht man natürlich auch die Kenntnis der globalen Entwicklungen, die Zwänge und Verführungen, die Trends und Moden, die Illusionen der Geschwindigkeiten, die geruchlose digitale Bilderwelt, um den Duft des Cviček überhaupt achten zu können. Wir müssen uns weiterhin, so glaube ich, die Recherche vor Ort, die Geduld mit den Problemen, den Respekt vor Bedürfnissen und Konventionen, kurz, die Aufmerksamkeit aber auch Gelassenheit dem Leben gegenüber leisten.

Edvard Ravnikar
Hotel Creina
Kranj 1968–70

102

locations (such as the square-like extension of the old city centre of Kranj), closer to the present day and with an enlarged scope did something similar with the so-called genius loci, by combining all elements he found there with those that he added, to form a new unity.

And seen in this way, architecture can maybe really only be found in "underdeveloped places" nowadays (I intentionally leave the countries out of it) or rather: in cultural situations that can afford the luxury of slowness, perseverance, responsibility for the people, historical aware-ness, collective memory and a permanent reflection of their own standpoint. This, of course, also requires a knowledge of global developments, constraints and seductions, trends and fashions, illusions of speeds, the aroma-less digital world of images, in order to be able to appreciate the aroma of Cvicek at all. We have to continue, I think, to afford for ourselves research on location, patience in dealing with problems, respect for needs and conventions, in short, to treat ourselves to being attentive but also imperturbable with regard to life.

Hotel Creina in Kranj, 1970

Ich habe zufällig den Zettel gefunden mit den handschriftlichen Mitteilungen Ravnikars, die er mir zum Hotel Creina mit auf den Weg gab. Wenn solche Angaben vielleicht auch wenig entschlüsseln, sind sie doch als dokumentarische Aussagen nicht uninteressant.

Hotel „Creina" in Kranj, 25 km nördlich von Ljubljana, einer Stadt von 18.000 Einwohnern und eine relativ reiche Stadt (Einkom. .... unleserlich) Elektro-, Textilindustrie und Tourismus.

Vor dem alten Stadttor hat sich in den letzten 10 Jahren ein großräumiges neues Zentrum zu entwickeln begonnen, leider nur in Stücken und vorläufig noch durch die Transitstraße Villach-Ljubljana sehr gestört.

Die Lage ist akzentuiert, der Bau liegt mit dem „Gesicht" gegen das Tal der Sava und gegen das Massiv eines bewaldeten Berges. Der Bau entwickelt sich im Schnitt in einer Höhe von (Angabe ausgelassen)
Die Grundidee war die unteren Räume die der Stadt gehören maximal zu öffnen, die Zimmer dagegen als „Anhalte für Vögel" oben in den Baumkronen zu verteilen.

Materiale: Sichtbeton, Ziegel, Holz und Textilbekleidung bei den Decken und Leuchtkörpern. Die ganze Anlage ist möglichst offen gedacht. Durch die Terrasse führt die Stadtmauerpromenade, die aber rechts und links noch angeschlossen ist.

Darf man bei dieser Fassadenzeichnung an Frank Lloyd Wright und ein wenig auch an Richard Neutra denken?

103

Autograph Ravnikar
„Hotel Creina"
1970

Hotel Creina in Kranj, 1970

By chance I found the piece of paper with the hand-written notes on the Creina Hotel Ravnikar gave me to take along. Even if such information may decipher only a few things, it still contains not uninteresting documentary information.

Hotel „Creina" in Kranj, 25 km north of Ljubljana, a city of 18,000 inhabitants and a relatively richt city (income ....illegible) electric-, textile industries and tourism.
Over the last 10 years an extensive new centre began to develop in front of the old city gate, unfortunately only in pieces and for the time being still heavily disturbed by the Villach-Ljubljana transit road.

The position is accentuated , the building "faces" the Sava valley and the massif of a wooded mountain. The building reaches an average height of (data omitted).
The basic idea was to create a maximum openness of the lower rooms which pertain to the city and to distribute the rooms by contrast as "stops for the birds" up in the treetops.

Materials: exposed concrete, brickwork, wood and textile cover of the ceilings and light sources. The entire complex is conceived to offer maximum openness. The city wall promenade which continues to the left and right nevertheless leads across the terrace.

Is it permitted to think of Frank Lloyd Wright and a bit also of Richard Neutra when watching this drawing of the façade?

ÜBER EDVARD RAVNIKAR

Mit der schlichten Metapher „Anhalte für Vögel" umschreibt Ravnikar ein sehr komplexes Thema einer Tourismusarchitektur: Es geht ja nicht nur um das Problem, reisenden Menschen eine gute Schlafstätte zu schaffen, sondern ihnen auch einen unvergesslichen Ort anzubieten. Seine Reaktion auf die städtebauliche Situation, auf die Terrassenkante vor der tieferliegenden Save, dem gegenüberliegenden grünen Berg, im Rücken einer Altstadt, ist ja mehr als ein Eingehen auf einen Ort, sie wertet diesen enorm auf, stellt ihn auch aus, um ihn den Gehirnen der flüchtig Anwesenden einzuprägen. Reisen im touristischen Kontext ist ja ein Sammeln von Eindrücken von Landschaften und Kulturen. Und da muss man den Gästen schon die schönsten Plätze mit der schönsten Aussicht anbieten, etwa in den Kronen der Bäume. Das ist nicht einfache Bedarfsdeckung, das ist Liebe zu einem Ort ausgedrückt mit den Mitteln des Bauens.

Niemand wird behaupten können, dass die kühne Stahlbetonkonstruktion nicht auf der Höhe der Zeit war, dass aber Ravnikar gleichzeitig mit einer der ältesten Bauweisen, dem Ziegel, eine handwerkliche Pracht entfaltet, eine fesselnde Bekleidung, die von der Struktur in eine Textur überleitet, die dann in einer ganz anderen Weise im Inneren mit Textilien eingelöst wird, ist nicht nur ein sinnliches Ereignis, sondern bringt Erinnerungen an einen tiefen Zeitraum mediterraner, ja orientalischer Kulturen ins Bewusstsein. Neues kann nur wahrgenommen werden, wenn es zu Altem in Kontakt tritt. Und hier wären wie wieder bei Josef Plečnik.

With the simple metaphor "stops for birds" Ravnikar paraphrases the very complex subject of architecture for tourism: the problem not only consists in creating a good place for travellers to sleep, but to also offer them an unforgettable place. His reaction to the topographic situation of the site, to the edge of the terrace in front of the lower-lying Sava and the green mountain opposite with the old city behind it, is much more than dealing with a location, it increases its value enormously, exposes it in order to make a lasting impression on the brief visitors. Tourism-related travelling is a gathering of impressions of landscapes and cultures. And under these circumstances, the guests have to be offered the most beautiful places with the finest views, for example, in the treetops. This is not simply fulfilling needs, this is love of a place expressed through building.

Nobody will claim that the bold reinforced concrete structure was not up to date, but at the same time Ravnikar uses one of the oldest construction materials, bricks, to reveal the splendor of the craft, a fascinating cover leading from structure to texture which is, in a quite different way, continued inside using textiles, thereby creating not only a sensual event but recalling long-gone memories of Mediterranean or even oriental cultures. New things can only be perceived when they come into contact with old things. Which brings us back to Josef Plečnik.

EDVARD RAVNIKAR: „FAST ALLES IST ARCHITEKTUR"
Begegnungen mit Edvard Ravnikar
EDVARD RAVNIKAR: "ALMOST EVERYTHING IS ARCHITECTURE"
Meetings with Edvard Ravnikar

FRIEDRICH KURRENT

Edvard Ravnikar (rechts) mit | with
Friedrich Achleitner (left)
am 1. Österreichischen Architekturkongress
1st Austrian Architectural congress
Payerbach, November 1970

*Dieser Text ist Teil eines Vortrages vom
Symposium in Ljubljana
am 3. und 4. Dezember 2007*

*The present text is part of a lecture held
at the symposium in Ljubljana,
on 3rd and 4th of December, 2007*

Diese Feststellung Ravnikars, vor beinahe vierzig Jahren ausgesprochen, reagierte damals vermutlich auf den autistisch-triumphierenden Slogan des Wiener Architekten Hans Hollein: „Alles ist Architektur".

Ravnikar hat diesen Slogan in ein Bonmot mit größerem Wahrheitsgehalt abgewandelt. Dieses lässt für weitere Überlegungen größeren Spielraum, lässt *fast* alles zu, ist aber nicht *alles*.

Typisch Ravnikar, schalkhaft zwinkernd; gegen alles Apodiktische.

Ravnikar war ein sokratisch Fragender, kaum in sein Inneres Einblick Gewährender.

Unser Freund Sokratis Dimitriou[1] meinte, Ravnikar sei ein byzantinischer Mensch, man könne seine geheime Welt nie ganz ergründen; hätte man eine Tür geöffnet, so wären weitere verschlossene da; selbst mit noch so vielen Schlüsseln könne man sein Inneres nie „aufsperren".

Wie gesagt, Ravnikar war ein Fragender.

Mit Fragen brachte er seine Studenten, auch seine Freunde zum Nachdenken, zum Überlegen, ja sogar zum Raten. Dies ging bei ihm bis zu Banalitäten.

Einmal fragte er im Kreise von Architekturstudenten und -studentinnen: „Was ist das wichtigste Architekturbuch?"

Die Antworten auf diese Rätselfrage reichten von Vitruv über Alberti, Palladio zu Le Corbusier oder Frank Lloyd Wright, schlussendlich zu Giedions „Space, Time and Architecture".

Bei allen Nennungen schüttelte Ravnikar verneinend sein eindrucksvolles Haupt.

Ravnikar made this statement almost forty years ago, probably as a reaction to the autistic triumphant slogan of the Viennese architect Hans Hollein: "Everything is architecture".

Ravnikar changed this slogan into a "bon mot" revealing a greater truth. It leaves more space for further reflection, includes *almost* everything, yet not *everything*.

Typically Ravnikar, roguish and with a wink; against anything apodictic.

Ravnikar was a Socratic questioner, scarcely allowing a glimpse into his inner life.

Our friend Sokratis Dimitriou[1] said Ravnikar was a Byzantine person whose secret world could never be entirely fathomed; if one door was opened, one would find others closed; no matter how many keys one used, his inner life could never be "unlocked".

As we said, Ravnikar was a questioner.

His questions made his students and also his friends think, reflect, even guess. He pursued this even with banalities.

He once asked his architecture students: "Which is the most important book of architecture?"

The answers to this riddle ranged from Vitruvius to Alberti, Palladio, Le Corbusier or Frank Lloyd Wright, finally to Giedion's "Space, Time and Architecture".

To all suggestions Ravnikar shook his impressive head.

1 Sokratis Dimitriou, 1919–1999;
Mitbegründer der Österreichischen
Gesellschaft für Architektur, Herausgeber
der Zeitschriften *Der Aufbau* und *Bauforum*; Professor für Kunstgeschichte
am Institut für Baukunst der TU Graz.

1 Sokratis Dimitriou, 1919–1999; co-founder
of the Austrian Society for architecture,
editor of the journals *Der Aufbau* and *Bauforum*; professor for history of art in Graz.

Dann kam seine Antwort: „NEUFERT – no, der Neufert." Neuferts Bauentwurfslehre sei das wichtigste Architekturbuch, sagte er. Auf allen Zeichentischen in allen Architekturbüros aller Länder läge es, in alle Sprachen wäre es übersetzt und publiziert; der „Neufert" werde überall von allen Entwerfern befragt; dort erfahre man die Maßbeziehungen, den Platzbedarf für die verschiedensten Bauaufgaben; seine System-Darstellungen seien international vermittelbar; im „Neufert" werde nachgeschlagen; auf den „Neufert" könne kein Architekt verzichten.

An Edvard Ravnikar erinnere ich mich anhand sechsmaliger persönlicher Begegnungen:

1. Als wir in Wien im Jahre 1967 die erste Plečnik-Ausstellung im deutschsprachigen Raum zeigten, veranstaltet von der kurz zuvor, 1965, gegründeten „Österreichischen Gesellschaft für Architektur", zum Gedächtnis des 10. Todestages des slowenischen Giganten – vor 40 Jahren also – war Ravnikar bald da. Podrecca hatte ihn eingeladen.
Damals kamen auch Marjan Mušič und France Stelé, um sich die Wiener Ausstellung anzusehen. (Sie ist übrigens bei der Niederwerfung des Prager Frühlings dort 1968 verschwunden.)

108

Then came his answer: "NEUFERT – well, the Neufert". Neufert's Architect's Data was the most important book of architecture, he said. It is to be found on all drawing boards in all architecture studios in all countries, it has been translated and published in all languages; the "Neufert" is consulted everywhere and by all designers; in it one finds out about dimensional relations, space requirements for different building tasks; its system representations are internationally communicable; everybody consults the "Neufert"; no architect can do without it.

I remember meeting Edvard Ravnikar personally six times:

1. When we showed the first Plečnik exposition in a German speaking country in 1967 in Vienna, organised by the "Austrian Society for Architecture" which had been founded a short time before, to commemorate the 10th death anniversary of the Slovenian giant – 40 years ago that is – Ravnikar was there. Podrecca had invited him.
Marjan Mušič and Francis Stelé had also come to visit the Viennese exposition. (It disappeared in Prague during the suppression of the Prague Spring in 1968, by the way.) This year a strange bond links Plečnik with Ravnikar: Plečnik's 50th death anniversary has been commemorated and now we are commemorating Ravnikar's 100th birthday.

Ein merkwürdiges Band verbindet im heurigen Jahr Plečnik mit Ravnikar: Plečniks 50. Todestags wurde gedacht, und nun gedenken wir Ravnikars 100. Geburtstags.

Meine Voraussage anlässlich der Münchner Plečnik-Ausstellung 1987, „Plečniks Werken werden starke und immer stärkere Flügel wachsen, mit denen sie den Aufstieg in die Zeitlosigkeit vollbringen werden", hat sich in den letzten Jahrzehnten weltweit erfüllt. Wir werden sehen, ob Ravnikars Lebenswerk im Laufe weiterer Jahre den Olymp vollends erklimmt?

2. Beim TRIGON-Wettbewerb der Nachbarländer Österreich, Italien, Jugoslawien 1969 in Graz waren wir beide zusammen mit dem Schweizer Max Bill, mit Franca Helg (der Partnerin von Franco Albini) aus Mailand, mit dem in den USA lebenden Grazer Friedrich St. Florian und dem Leiter der „Neuen Galerie der Stadt Graz" Wilfried Skreiner Juroren beim Wettbewerb „Architektur und Freiheit". Damals wurde der titelgebende Satz „Fast alles ist Architektur" ausgesprochen. Ravnikar hatte bei der Auswahl ein gutes Gespür für sensible Projekte.

Im Trigon-Katalog schrieb Ravnikar einen kurzen Text „Architektur und Freiheit" („Arhitektura in Svoboda"), da lesen wir u. a.:

„... Der Zweck als Sinn unseres Handelns auf dem Architekturgebiet schließt rationale und auch irrationale Werte ein. Die ersten sind messbar, allgemein zugänglich und leicht beschreibbar. Die anderen hingegen bleiben meistens verborgen ...

My prediction on the occasion of the Plečnik exposition in Munich in 1987, "The wings on Plečnik's works will ever grow stronger, allowing them to rise to timelessness" has proven true all over the world during the last decades. In the course of time we will see whether Ravnikar's life's work will succeed in climbing all the way up to Mount Olympus.

2. At the TRIGON competition of the neighbouring countries Austria, Italy and Yugoslavia in 1969 in Graz we were both jurors in the "architecture and freedom" competition together with the Swiss Max Bill, with Franca Helg (the partner of Franco Albini) from Milan, with Friedrich St. Florian from Graz who lives in the USA and the director of the "New Gallery of the City of Graz", Wilfried Skreiner. It was on that occasion the words quoted in the title "Almost everything is architecture" were spoken. In his selection Ravnikar had a feeling for sensitive projects. In the Trigon catalogue Ravnikar wrote a short text "Architecture and Freedom" stating:

"...The purpose of our activities in the field of architecture encompasses rational and also irrational values. The former are measurable, generally accessible and easy to describe. The latter, however, remain mostly hidden...

... Die Freiheit an sich ist ein abstrakter Begriff, wenn man frei sein will, muss man frei von etwas sein können. Der Mensch braucht eigentlich einen Komplex von einzelnen Freiheiten, welche für jeden von uns die allgemeine Freiheit bedeuten. Eine gut organisierte Stadt macht frei von provinzieller Hoffnungslosigkeit. Die eigene Wohnung macht frei von Bedrängtsein durch die soziale Umgebung usw."

3. Im Dezember des Jahres 1970 veranstaltete die Österreichische Gesellschaft für Architektur den dreitägigen „Ersten österreichischen Architekturkongress" zu den hundertsten Geburtstagen von Adolf Loos und Josef Hoffmann (die nur 5 Tage auseinander liegen: Loos 10. 12. 1870; Hoffmann 15. 12. 1870), und zwar im von Loos und Heinrich Kulka 1930 erbauten Berghaus (Khuner), der heutigen „Pension Alpenhof" in Payerbach am Semmering.
Ravnikar war einer der eingeladenen ausländischen Gäste und machte manchmal kryptische Bemerkungen.

4. Im Oktober 1971 unternahmen wir als Architekturgesellschaft eine Slowenien-Reise. Freilich standen Plečniks Bauten an erster Stelle der Besichtigungen; in Bogojina fingen wir damit an. Als wir abends mit dem Bus in Ljubljana eintrafen, erwartete uns die Gruppe mit France Stelé, Ravnikar, dem Plečnik-Mitarbeiter Tone Bitenc, dem jungen Kunsthistoriker Damjan

... Freedom as such is an abstract concept, if you want to be free, you have to be able to be free of something. Man actually needs a complex of individual freedoms, which for each of us mean general freedom. A well organised city offers freedom from provincial despair. Having one's own apartment liberates from oppression by the social environment, etc."

3. In December of the year 1970, the Austrian Society for Architecture organised the 3-day "First Austrian Congress of Architecture" on the hundredth birthdays of Adolf Loos and Josef Hoffmann (which are only 5 days apart: Loos 10. 12. 1870; Hoffmann 15. 12. 1870) at the Berghaus (Khuner) which had been designed and built by Loos and Heinrich Kulka in 1930, known today as "Pension Alpenhof" in Payerbach on the Semmering.
Ravnikar was among the invited foreign guests and sometimes made cryptic remarks.

4. In October, 1971, we made a trip to Slovenia as the Society of Architecture. Plečnik's buildings were of course the first to be visited; we started in Bogojina. When we arrived in the evening by bus in Ljubljana, a group including Francis Stelé, Ravnikar, the Plečnik-cooperator Tone Bitenc, the young art historian Damjan Prelovšek awaited us at the Prešeren memorial. The next day we visited the most important Plečnik buildings. Ravnikar was very reserved, almost shy when he presented his own buildings, which were mostly residential.

Prelovšek beim Prešeren-Denkmal. Am nächsten Tag wurden die wichtigsten Plečnik-Bauten besichtigt. Ravnikar war beim Zeigen seiner eigenen Bauten, meist Wohnbauten, sehr zurückhaltend, fast schüchtern.

Den Abend verbrachten wir bei Zwitschek mit unseren slowenischen neuen Freunden in einer Laibacher Weinlaube. Den melodiösen Klang der deutsch sprechenden Slowenen habe ich heute noch im Ohr.

Selbst war ich schon vorher einmal, 1963, (mit Maria) auf Plečniks Spuren in Laibach; war aber noch nicht genügend über sein Spätwerk informiert.

Obwohl ich den Architekten Ravnikar noch nicht kannte, nichts über ihn wusste, fiel mir damals das von ihm gebaute Druckereigebäude bzw. das Büro- und Geschäftshaus in der Nähe der Drachenbrücke, nicht weit von Plečniks Bügeleisenhaus auf. Diese konstruktiv-tektonische Klarheit war damals für uns genau das, was wir in der Architektur anstrebten.

Im Erdgeschoss befand sich eine Buchhandlung, in der ich vergeblich nach Plečnik-Literatur suchte, aber immerhin ein Buch von Neidhardt & Grabrijan fand.

Zurück zur Slowenien-Exkursion: am übernächsten Tag führte uns Ravnikar nach Istrien, nach Piran und Poreč, nach Motovun, Grožnjan, Hrastovlje. Da war Ravnikar in seinem Element: Die Adria, das Venezianische, der Karst waren sein lokaler Hintergrund, sein Territorium.

111

We spent the evening drinking Cviček with our new Slovenian friends in a Ljubljana wine bar. I can still remember the melodious sound of the German speaking Slovenians.

I had already followed Plečnik's tracks in Ljubljana earlier, in 1963, (with Mary), but I had not been sufficiently informed about his late works.

Although I was not yet familiar with the architect Ravnikar, knew nothing about him, the printers' building designed by him as well as the office building near the Dragon Bridge, not far from Plečnik's Flat Iron Building attracted my attention. It was exactly this type of structural tectonic clarity that we were striving for in architecture.

On the ground floor there was a book shop in which I looked in vain for literature on Plečnik, but at least found a book by Neidhardt & Grabrijan.

Back to the Slovenian excursion: on the third day Ravnikar took us to Istria, to Piran and Poreč, to Motovun, Grožnjan, Hrastovlje. There Ravnikar was on home turf. The Adriatic, the Venetian influence, the karst were his local background, his territory.

On the fourth day, the day of our return journey, Ravnikar showed us his latest buildings in Kranj: The "Creina" hotel, a reinforced concrete building with exposed brickwork panelling and impressive interior spaces, and the entirely different "Globus" department store. We also visited the municipality building with the vaulted roof built ten years earlier.

Ravnikar's buildings showed equally constructional-structural clarity, enormous feeling for materials and subtle furnishings.

Am vierten Tag, am Tag der Rückreise, zeigte uns Ravnikar seine jüngsten Bauten in Kranj: Das Hotel „Creina", ein Stahlbetonbau mit Sichtziegelausfachung und eindrucksvoller Innenräumlichkeit und das völlig anders geartete Kaufhaus „Globus". Auch das zehn Jahre ältere Stadtverwaltungsgebäude mit dem bombierten Dach besichtigten wir. Ravnikars Bauten zeigten gleichermaßen konstruktiv-strukturelle Klarheit, enormes Materialgefühl und subtile Ausstattungsqualität.

5. Um 1980 fand das Preisgericht zur Grazer Opernerweiterung statt, bei dem Ravnikar und ich mit anderen Preisrichtern Juroren waren. Ravnikar hatte das „Cankarjev dom", das Laibacher Kultur- und Kongresszentrum in Arbeit, und dadurch wertvolle Erfahrungen im Theater- und Bühnenbau. Wawrik gewann.

6. Am 17. Februar 1981 hielt Ravnikar an der Technischen Universität in München einen Gastvortrag über das illegale Bauen in Slowenien („Crne gradnje sloveniji"). Ich erinnere mich, dass an meiner Architekturfakultät als Vortragsankündigung der Titel „Die schwarzen Häuser Sloweniens" plakatiert war. Ich hatte das Vergnügen, Ravnikar in München vorzustellen.
Über diese geschilderten Begegnungen hinaus, die von den sechziger bis in die achtziger Jahre des vorigen Jahrhunderts reichten, wissen wir inzwischen mehr, besonders durch die

112

5. Around 1980 I was on a jury for the enlargement of the opera house in Graz together with Ravnikar. He was working at the "Cankarjev dom", the cultural and congress centre in Ljubljana and had gathered valuable experience in theatre and stage construction. Wawrik won.

6. On February 17th, 1981, Ravnikar gave a guest lecture at the University of Technology in Munich on the subject of illegal building in Slovenia. I remember that at my faculty of architecture the lecture was announced on posters as "The Black Houses of Slovenia". I had the pleasure of introducing Ravnikar in Munich.

We now know more than what I have related about these encounters which took place between the 60s and 80s of the last century, particularly thanks to the publication "Hommage à Edvard Ravnikar 1907–1993", edited and compiled by France Ivanšek.

Publikation „Hommage à Edvard Ravnikar 1907–1993", herausgegeben und zusammenge-
stellt von France Ivanšek.

Ravnikar hat 1991 die Eigenstaatlichkeit Sloweniens gerade noch erlebt.

Ich habe an Ravnikar nie eine nationalistische Einstellung entdeckt. Er schien mir ein Welt-
mann, ein Weltbürger, ein Kosmopolit zu sein, ein Europäer, ein weltläufiger Europäer, der
sich in allen Ländern und Städten, in Venedig und Triest, genauso gut wie in Wien und Paris
verständigen konnte und sich souverän bewegte.

Als junger Mann hat Ravnikar bekanntlich 4 Jahre, von 1926–1930, in Wien studiert; dann
absolvierte er in Ljubljana bei Plečnik sein Architekturstudium und diplomierte 1935; im ersten
Halbjahr 1939 hat er bei Le Corbusier in Paris gearbeitet.

Vorher noch hat er 1937–1939 in Žale den Rundbau für die Gefallenen des Ersten Weltkriegs
errichtet – noch ganz in Abhängigkeit von Plečniks Sakralbau-Architektur.

Ravnikars Rundbau | rotunda in Žale

Seine Laibacher „Moderne Galerie" beim Tivoli fiel in die Zerreißprobe Plečnik – Le Corbusier.
Im Baukörper entdeckte ich Otto-Wagnerisches, in den Wandoberflächen einen Nachhall der
Plečnik-Schule, aber auch schon anklingende Corbu-Elemente, zum Beispiel beim Vordach.

Durch Plečniks Erbe war Ravnikar noch im Besitz des Ornamentalen, dieses wurde von
Le Corbusier abgeräumt. Ravnikars spätere subtile Material- und Detailbehandlung hat

113

Ravnikar saw Slovenia gain its sovereignty in 1991 only a short time before his death.
I never detected a nationalist attitude in Ravnikar. He appeared as a man of the world, a
citizen of the world, a cosmopolitan European who could communicate in all countries and
cities, in Venice and Trieste as well as in Vienna and Paris, and who had a commanding
knowledge of his subject.

As you may know, Ravnikar studied in Vienna for 4 years as a young man, between 1926
and 1930; then continued his architectural studies in Ljubljana with Plečnik and earned his
diploma in 1935; during the first half of 1939 he worked with Le Corbusier in Paris.

Before that, he built the rotunda for the fallen soldiers of the 1st World War in Žale in
1937–1939 – still wholly depending on Plečnik's style of sacred architecture.

Ravnikars Moderne Galerie | Modern Gallery

His "Modern Gallery" in Ljubljana near the Tivoli reveals an inner conflict between Plečnik
and Le Corbusier. In the structure of the building I discovered reminiscences of Otto Wagner,
on the wall surfaces an echo of the Plečnik-school, but also a hint of Corbu-elements such as
the canopy.

Through Plečnik's inheritance Ravnikar was still in possession of the ornamental; this was
cleared away by Le Corbusier. Ravnikar's later subtle handling of material and details kept
fragments thereof alive, albeit in a covert, almost invisible way as it seems to me, presented
to the eye and to the haptic faculties. Ravnikar renounced ornamental-decorative forms.

unterirdisch, fast unsichtbar, wie mir scheint, doch noch solche Fragmente lebendig erhalten, dem Auge und dem Haptischen dargeboten. Ravnikar verzichtete auf ornamental-dekorative Erscheinungsformen.

Mit großer Phantasie und mithilfe kongenialer Bauingenieure entwickelte er seine konstruktiven Maßnahmen, die jeder dekorativen Komponente abhold waren.

Die Beendigung des Zweiten Weltkriegs muss, ähnlich in Österreich, ein großes Aufatmen gewesen sein. Schon um 1940 schälte sich aus der Plečnik-Corbusier-Architektur die Ravnikar-Architektur heraus, die in den nächsten fünf Jahrzehnten sein Bauen bestimmte; da hatte er sich als Architekt selbst gefunden.

Krönender Abschluss wurde sein Alters-Bauwerk, die Stadtmitte Laibachs am Revolutions-, heute Republiks-Platz. Damit gab er dem alten römischen EMONA (Emona = hebräisch: Glaube) zu Ende des 20. Jahrhunderts die moderne Stadtmitte.

Schon in frühen Skizzen sehen wir eine Doppeltürmigkeit, zuerst noch kubisch, ab 1960 im Grundplan dreiecksförmig, anfangs noch zwei Seiten des gleichseitigen Dreiecks parallel gestellt und plötzlich in den Siebzigerjahren gedreht, sodass sich zwei abgekantete Spitzen des Dreiecks gegenüberstehen – ein Genieblitz!

114

With a lot of imagination and with the support of perfectly matched construction engineers he developed his structural measures averse to any decorative component.

The end of World War II must have been a great relief, as it was in Austria. As early as 1940 Plečnik-Corbusier-architecture gave way to Ravnikar architecture which for the next five decades determined his building activity; he had come into his own as an architect.

The culmination was his later building, the city centre of Ljubljana on the Square of the Revolution – today the Square of the Republic. He hereby equipped the former Roman EMONA (emona = Hebrew: faith) in the late 20th century with a modern city centre.
In early sketches we already see a twin-tower-shape, first cubic, after 1960 with a triangular layout, in the beginning still with two sides of the equilateral triangle in parallel arrangement and suddenly, in the 70s, turned so that two bevelled points of the triangle are arranged opposite each other – a stroke of genius!

The wind coming from the Karawanken over the plain to the Ljubljana castle can now whistle through this narrow pass.

Ljubljana mit den Karawanken |
with the Karawanken

Jetzt kann der Wind von den Karawanken kommend, über die Ebene, bis zur Laibacher Burg durch diese Engstelle pfeifen. Die Türme stehen sich wie Magneten gegenüber und setzen das Platz-Ensemble unter „Strom". Es könnte schiefgehen, in ein altes Stadtzentrum Hochhäuser zu bauen, wie dies in Wien vor vier Jahren mit den Türmen „Wien-Mitte" drohte; diese sollten, nur 800 Meter vom Stephansturm entfernt, gebaut werden.

Die Mitte der Stadt war aber schon da: der Stephansturm, mit seinen 137 Metern Höhe. Hier in Laibach hingegen stimmt das Konzept. Ravnikars Spürsinn für den jeweiligen Ort ist bewunderns- wert. Was der Ort sagt, wird erhört, oder er wird durch bauliche Setzung zu einem solchen ge- macht. Edvard Ravnikar war nicht nur ein großer Architekt, sondern auch ein großer Städtebauer. Vieles wäre noch anzusprechen, etwa: Ravnikar der Zeichner. Nicht nur seine Plangraphik ist zu einer persönlichen Ausdrucksweise geworden, sondern und besonders seine freien Zeich- nungen, Skizzen sind visuelle Gustostückerl. Seine charakteristischen diagonal-gekreuzten Schraffuren vermitteln räumliche Atmosphäre – analoge Zeichnungen, wie sie die digitale Ma- schine nicht hervorbringen kann.

Sie hören, ich bin ein unverbesserlicher Analoger, die hiesigen Veranstalter hatten ihre liebe Not mit mir: kein Handy, kein Fax, kein E-Mail; nur Telephon, der alte Brief und die Zugverbin- dung. Aber ich glaube – auch ohne mediale Hilfsmittel – an Ravnikars Behauptung
FAST ALLES IST ARCHITEKTUR.

The towers face each other like magnets and electrify the square ensemble. Things could eas- ily go wrong when you build high-rises in an old city centre as almost happened in Vienna four years ago when the "Wien-Mitte" towers were planned only 800 meters from St. Stephen's Cathedral. In the latter case the centre of the city was already there: St. Stephen's steeple, 137 metres high. But here in Ljubljana the concept fit. Ravnikar's instinct for each particular location is admirable. He responds to what the place is saying or intervenes through his architecture to make it speak.

Edvard Ravnikar was not only a great architect, but alto a great town planner.

Much more would have to be addressed, for example: Ravnikar's drawings. Not only the artwork of his architectural drawings have become a personal mode of expression, but also and above all his free drawings, his sketches are visual delicacies. His characteristic diagonal cross hatching conveys a spatial atmosphere – analogous drawings that cannot be produced by the digital machine.

As you have undoubtedly noticed, I am incorrigibly analogous, the local organizers had a hard time with me: no mobile phone, no fax machine, no e-mail; only the telephone, the old snail mail and railroad connection. But I believe – also without the aid of media – in Ravnikar's statement ALMOST EVERYTHING IS ARCHITECTURE.

IN RICHTUNG EINER GENERATION OHNE MEISTER
Die vielfältigen Seelen der zeitgenössischen slowenischen Architektur
TOWARDS A GENERATION WITHOUT A MASTER
The manifold souls of contemporary Slovenian architecture

LUKA SKANSI

Architekt, Architekturhistoriker | Architect, Architectural historian
Ljubljana / Venedig | Venice

Sadar Vuga
Handelskammer
Sloweniens
Chamber of Commerce
and Industry of Slovenia
Ljubljana 1996–99

Eine Überlegung zur architektonischen Produktion der letzten Jahre in Slowenien bedeutet, die wichtigsten Paradigmen ausfindig zu machen, die die jüngere europäische Architektur im Allgemeinen charakterisieren. Nicht um zu zeigen, wie „reif" und international das Architekturschaffen in diesem Lande ist – eine Eigenschaft, die es ohnehin über das ganze 20. Jahrhundert ausgezeichnet hat – sondern eher, um innerhalb eines weiter gefassten und komplexeren Kontextes die Qualität wie auch die Inkohärenz der heutigen Baupraxis zu charakterisieren.

Nach 17 Jahren Unabhängigkeit ist die architektonische Kultur Sloweniens von allgemeinen Bedingungen gekennzeichnet, die typisch für den Berufsstand in der westlichen Welt sind. Die Notwendigkeit, seine Kompetenzen laufend auf wirtschaftliche und administrative Abläufe auszuweiten, die Industrialisierung und Standardisierung im Bau, die Bedeutung des Marketings und das Streben nach Mediatisierung – all das sind Gründe für die wesentlichen Veränderungen, die die Praxis der slowenischen Architekturateliers in den letzten zwei Jahrzehnten geprägt haben.

Die daraus resultierende zunehmende Komplexität des Berufs entwickelt sich parallel zu einer Welle der kulturellen und sprachlichen Nivellierung, die bereits alle Bereiche des Kunstschaffens erfasst hat. Die massive Mediatisierung bewirkte ab Mitte der 90er Jahre eine Globalisierung der Architektur (es kam zur Verbreitung neuer „internationaler Stile"), verbunden mit der Verringerung von Qualität und Lehre an den Hochschulen – bei gleichzeitiger Homogenisierung der architektonischen Suche – sowie dem Trend, internationale Postdiplomstudien zu absolvie-

Careful consideration of the architectural production of the last years in Slovenia involves analysis of the main paradigms characterizing young European architecture in general. Not in order to show how "mature" and international architectural production is in this country – a feature which characterized it throughout the 20th century anyway – but rather to define the quality and inconsistency of today's construction practice within a wider and more complex context.

After 17 years of independence, the architectural culture of Slovenia is characterized by general conditions which are typical for the profession all over the whole world. The need to continuously expand one's competencies to include economic and administrative developments, definitive industrialization and standardization in construction, the importance of marketing and the tendency towards mediatization – all these are the causes of the changes that have taken place in Slovenian architecture studios in the last two decades.

The resulting increasing complexity of the profession is a parallel development to a wave of cultural and linguistic levelling which has already seized all areas of artistic creation. Massive mediatization provoked a globalisation of architecture starting in the mid 90s (the spread of new "international styles"), combined with a reduction in the quality of teaching at the universities – with simultaneous homogenisation of the architectural quest – and the trend to enrol in international post-diploma studies. According architects, the search for an architectural "identity", the study of form that reflects the relationship to certain places and traditions

ren. Die Suche nach einer architektonischen „Identität", die Studie der Form, die Beziehungen zu bestimmten Orten und Traditionen widerspiegelt, erscheint nach Ansicht der Architekten immer weniger erstrebenswert. Besonders die jüngste Generation, für die der Begriff Tradition – bedingt durch die Faszination des internationalen „Star-Systems" – einen negativen Beigeschmack hat, wird sie als Hindernis auf dem Weg zur Anerkennung durch Medien und Berufswelt gesehen. All das wird von einer Vereinheitlichung der Sprache begleitet, die von einem digitalen Dekorativismus produziert wird: Dieser bietet ewig „Neues" und erinnert den Betrachter an die spektakulären aber verbrauchten grafischen Gesten der Stararchitektur.

Diese Problemkreise – komplexe Baupraxis, neue Auftragsstrukturen, architektonische Sprache zwischen Tradition und Internationalismus – bilden den Hintergrund für eine Betrachtung des Bauens in Slowenien. Es ist eine besonders interessante Zeit, charakterisiert von einer vielfältigen Produktion, wie sie kaum in einem anderen europäischen „Übergangs"-Land vorkommt. Diese fruchtbare Zeit ist gekennzeichnet von neuen Aufgaben für die Architektur in der Phase des wirtschaftlichen Aufschwungs und der politischen Veränderungen in Slowenien als Folge der Auflösung Jugoslawiens und des Übergangs zur Demokratie. Diese Aufgaben haben – in völlig ungewöhnlicher Weise – vor allem die neuen Generationen bekommen, sie haben die gefestigten Hierarchien überwunden, die sich in der jüngsten Vergangenheit gebildet hatten, sie haben sich als reif erwiesen – oder einfach als vorbereitet – der neuen Dynamik des Marktes zu entsprechen.

Oton Jugovec
„Baza 20"
Kočevski Rog 1986–88

118

seems less and less worthwhile. Particularly the youngest generation for whom the notion of tradition – due to the fascination of the international "star system" – has an unpleasant taste, sees it as an obstacle on the way to recognition by the media and the professional world. All this is accompanied by a standardization of language produced by a digital decorativism that is always coming up with something "new" and reminds the viewer of the spectacularely tired graphic gestures of star architecture.

These concerns – complex construction practice, new order structures, architectural language between tradition and internationalism – form the background of an analysis of architecture in Slovenia. It is a particularly interesting time, characterized by a variety of production that is hard to find in any other European "transition"-country. During this fertile period new tasks for architecture abounded at a time of economic upswing and of political changes in Slovenia as a result of the disintegration of Yugoslavia and the transition to democracy. These tasks were – in an entirely unusual way – given above all to the new generations, they overcame the consolidated hierarchies that had formed in the recent past, they proved to be sufficiently mature – or simply prepared – to face the new dynamics of the market.

Rok Klanjšček
„Nebesa" Berghütten
The "Nebesa" Tourist Mountain Retreat
Livek bei | near Kobarid 2003

Die neue Slowenische Wirtschaftskammer – ein Werk der Architekten Jure Sadar und Boštjan Vuga (beide noch keine 40) – markiert zweifellos den Beginn einer neuen Ära der slowenischen Architektur. Dieses 1999 fertig gestellte Gebäude wirkt durch das Potential, das es manifestiert, unmittelbar als starkes Signal für neue Generationen: Als Ergebnis eines Wettbewerbs wird der Bau einer der wichtigsten Institutionen des neuen Staates einem jungen und wenig bekannten Architekturatelier anvertraut, dem es gelingt, dem Gebäude einen spektakulären Ausdruck zu verleihen, der sich radikal von früheren Beispielen slowenischer Architektur unterscheidet. Eine Publikation aus Anlass der Fertigstellung beschreibt die generativen und konstruktiven Prozesse, die zum außergewöhnlichen Werk geführt haben, und trägt dazu bei, dass das Bauwerk zu einem wahren Medienevent wird.

Das Gebäude erscheint als explizite Negation des historisierenden und monumentalen Ästhetismus, der die slowenische Architektur der 80er Jahre charakterisiert, es importiert die – alles andere als neuen – neofunktionalistischen holländischen Ansätze in den slowenischen Kontext. Das generierende Element dieses Projekts ist der transitive Ausdruck der inneren Funktionen des Gebäudes auf die Gliederung seiner Fassaden und Volumen. Die beiden Trakte – Bürotrakt und öffentlicher Trakt – sind mit unterschiedlichen strukturellen und expressiven Systemen ausgestattet: räumlicher Raster in Stahl für die öffentlichen Bereiche, Schachtel aus Stahlbeton für die Büros. Dadurch wird ein zweifacher Effekt erzielt: flach und zweidimensional die

Ofis (Rok Oman, Spela Videčnik
„Hayrack" Wohnbau | residential building
Cerklje 2005–07

119

Sadar Vuga
Wohnbau | residential building
Nova Gorica 2004-07

The new building for the Chamber of Commerce and Industry of Slovenia that was designed by the architects Jure Sadar and Boštjan Vuga (both were younger at the time) – doubtlessly marks the begin of a new era in Slovenian architecture. Through the potential that it manifests, this building completed in 1999 is a powerful signal for new generations: as a result of having won the competition, the construction of one of the most important institutions of the new nation is awarded to a young and little known architecture studio which then succeeds in making the building spectacularly expressive, differing radically from earlier examples of Slovenian architecture. A publication on to celebrate its completion describes the generative and constructional processes that led to this extraordinary work and contributes to making the building a true media event.

The building appears as an explicit negation of the historicizing and monumental aestheticism so typical of Slovenian architecture in the 80s, it imports the – anything but new – neofunctionalist Dutch approaches and brings them into the Slovenian context. The generating element of this project is the transitive expression of the inner functions of the building onto the organisation of its façades and volumes. The two wings – office wing and public wing – are equipped with different structural and expressive systems: a three-dimensional steel pattern for the public areas, boxes of reinforced concrete for the offices. This creates a double effect: flat and two-dimensional backside of the building, deep and structured towards the square and the street – the intention is to achieve the most radical expression of what is happening inside.

Enota
Hotel Sotelia
Podčetrtek 2004–06

IN RICHTUNG EINER GENERATION OHNE MEISTER

Ausstellungskatalog
"6IX PACK. CONTEMPORARY SLOVENIAN
ARCHITECTURE" | Sechserpack. zeitge-
nössische slowenische Architektur
2003

Gebäuderückseite, tief und gegliedert zum Platz und zur Straße – dadurch soll das Thema der inneren Abläufe extrem radikalisiert werden. Die Möglichkeiten, die eine Stahlkonstruktion bietet, werden von Sadar-Vuga eingesetzt, um dem Gebäude eine suggestive Plastizität zu verleihen: vorspringende Teile und versetzte Volumen, Sprünge, Ausnehmungen und Füllungen im Raster. Über das Erzeugen einer neuen Sprache hinaus dient dieses Werk als Musterbeispiel für die Möglichkeiten einer Verschränkung von zeitgenössischer Architektur mit Institutionen und begleitet die Medien, besonders die nicht spezialisierten, in einem parallelen Prozess der Erzeugung einer „Lust" auf's Neue. Zur Zeit lässt sich eine Vielzahl von Zeitschriften, Kolumnen in den Tageszeitungen und Fernsehsendungen beobachten, die sich ausgiebig mit Architektur, Design und Einrichtung in Slowenien befassen; so werden diese Themen zum Gesprächsinhalt für ein breites Publikum. Dadurch kommen die Aufgaben der konsolidierten professionellen Kanäle (traditionelle Zeitschriften, die Rolle des Architektenverbandes, die Architekturschule von Ljubljana …) ins Hintertreffen, denen in gewisser Weise die Exklusivität und Autonomie der Verbreitung der zeitgenössischen Diskussion entzogen wird. Ein Prozess, der sicher beigetragen hat, Architektur zum Werbeträger und zu einem Gegenstand des breiteren Konsums zu machen, gleichzeitig kam es aber zu einer Verflachung der Diskussion sowie zur Reduktion ihrer Bedeutungen auf im Wesentlichen visuelle und inszenatorische Werte.

Ende der 90er Jahre entsteht – auch als Folge dieser Umstände – eine Vielzahl von jungen

The possibilities offered by a steel structure are used by Sadar-Vuga to lend the building suggestive plasticity: protruding elements and offset volumes, breaks, recesses and fillings in the pattern. Besides creating a new language, this work is also an example of how contemporary architecture and institutions can be combined and joins the media, particularly the not specialized media, in a parallel process creating a "desire" for something new. At present there are many journals, newspaper columns and TV programs in Slovenia that deal extensively with architecture, design and furnishings; so that these subjects have become the topic of conversation of a broad public and the tasks of the consolidated professional channels (traditional journals, the role of the architects' association, the school of architecture in Ljubljana,…) fall behind because to a certain extent they have lost their exclusive and autonomous rights to disseminate the contemporary discussion. This process has definitely contributed to turning architecture into an advertising medium and a subject of wider consumption, but at the same time the discussion has degenerated and the meaning of architecture has been reduced to mainly visual and theatrical aspects.

At the end of the 90s – partly as a result of these circumstances – a multitude of young studios were created which gained acceptance in the national scene both through their projects and their publications: first the Ateliers Bevk-Perović, Ofis, Dekleva-Gregorič studios, all graduates of important international schools (Berlage Institute Rotterdam and AA Lon-

Ateliers, die sich in der heimischen Szene durchsetzten, sei es mit Realisierungen, wie auch mit Publikationen: zunächst die Ateliers Bevk-Perović, Ofis, Dekleva-Gregorič, alle Absolventen von bedeutenden internationalen Ausbildungsstätten (Berlage Institute Rotterdam und AA London), in jüngerer Zeit die Gruppen Enota und Arhitektura Krušec. Diese Ateliers reihen sich in ein Panorama einer Entwicklung ein, das verschiedene Generationen von Architekten aus der Architekturschule von Ljubljana der 70er und 80er Jahre bilden: auf der einen Seite Vojteh Ravnikar, Aleš Vodopivec, Jurij Kobe, Janez Koželj, Miha Dešman – Architekten, die die Szene der 80er Jahre prägten, und die mit ihrer wertvollen editorischen und didaktischen Tätigkeit die nationale Kultur mit den interessantesten internationalen theoretischen und projektbezogenen Studien aktualisieren; auf der anderen Seite Matej und Vesna Vozlič, Andrej Kemr, Nande Korpnik, Miloš Florijančič, Janko Zadravec, die eine Generation von Professionisten verkörpern, die erst relativ spät – nach der Wirtschaftskrise der 80er Jahre – Gelegenheit hatte, sich zu behaupten. Daraus resultiert eine reichhaltige wie vielfältige Landschaft der zeitgenössischen slowenischen Architektur, die sich nur schwer in einzelne Tendenzen zusammenfassen lässt. Klar ist, dass diese Architekten den Schulen, Büro- und Industriegebäuden, Bibliotheken und Museen der letzten Jahre ihren Stempel aufgedrückt haben; außerdem sind sie Autoren von wichtigen Studien über Wohn- und Siedlungstypologien. Sowohl privaten wie öffentlichen Auftraggebern vermitteln sie den Eindruck, einen technischen und intellektuellen Status im heutigen Sloweni-

Magazin | Magazine 2G
Nr. 38 / 2006

122

don), more recently the groups Enota and Arhitektura Krušec. These studios are part of a panorama that includes different generations of architects from the School of Architecture of Ljubljana of the 70s and 80s: on the one hand, Vojteh Ravnikar, Aleš Vodopivec, Jurij Kobe, Janez Koželj, Miha Dešman – architects who pervaded the scene in the 80s and who by their valuable editorial and didactic activities updated the national culture with interesting international theoretical and project-related studies; on the other hand, Matej und Vesna Vozlič, Andrej Kemr, Nande Korpnik, Miloš Florijančič, Janko Zadravec, who stand for a generation of professionals which only relatively recently – after the economic crisis of the 80s – were able to gain acceptance. This brought us a rich and manifold landscape of contemporary Slovenian architecture which is difficult to summarize in individual tendencies. It is obvious that these architects left their mark on the schools, office and industrial buildings, libraries and museums of the last years; furthermore they are authors of important studies on housing and settlement typologies. To both private and public clients they convey the impression that they embody a technical and intellectual status in present Slovenia that exceeds the comparable European situation and they are actively engaged in the development of urban districts. Nevertheless it appears that their role is not sufficiently strong to even slightly reduce the gap between quality and victorious mediocrity – which is so typical for the uncontrolled growth of the cities –, and the discipline of architecture in Slovenia is becoming exactly that which it already is in other European contexts: an isolated and in a way elitist phenomenon.

en zu verkörpern, der vergleichbare europäischen Situationen übersteigt, und sie arbeiten aktiv an der Entwicklung von Stadtteilen mit. Dennoch erweist sich ihre Rolle als nicht ausreichend solide, um die Kluft zwischen Qualität und siegreicher Mittelmäßigkeit – die so typisch ist für die unkontrollierbare Wucherung der Städte – auch nur ein bisschen einzuschränken, und die Disziplin der Architektur wird in Slowenien genau zu dem, was sie in anderen europäischen Kontexten bereits ist: ein vereinzeltes und in gewisser Weise elitäres Phänomen.

Schließlich stellt sich die Frage der Kontinuität – oder anders gesagt, der Beziehung des heutigen Architekturschaffens zur Geschichte der slowenischen Architektur. Ein Thema, das nicht zu verwechseln ist mit jenem des Verhältnisses zum traditionellen Bauen oder zur historischen Struktur der Städte. De facto ist es gerade das 20. Jahrhundert, das in Slowenien den mächtigsten physischen Ausdruck der Städte und architektonischen Werke gebildet hat, was wiederum neue Traditionen erzeugt hat, die absolut bestimmend für das kulturelle und bauliche Erbe der Nation sind. Zu diesem Thema erweisen sich einige jüngere Arbeiten als besonders interessant: die France-Bevk-Bibliothek in Nova Gorica von Ravnikar-Potokar mit der Komplexität ihrer räumlichen Komposition und Grundrisskonzeption; der Friedhof Srebrniče von Vodopivec mit seinem raffinierten Konzeptualismus; das elegante Entwickeln der Details beim Linde-Gebäude des Ateliers Vozlič – alles bemerkenswerte Ansätze, wo die perzeptive Erfahrung der Werke früherer Meister und die neue Architektursprache eine Symbiose eingehen.

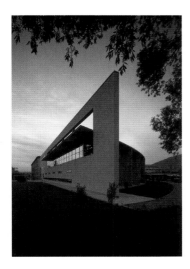

Vojteh Ravnikar, Robert Potokar,
Maruša Zorec
Öffentliche Bibliothek France Bevk
Public Library France Bevk
Nova Gorica 1995–2000

Finally we have to address the question of continuity – or in other words, the relationship between today's architectural production and the history of Slovenian architecture. A subject which must not be necessarily correlated with the relationship to traditional building or to the historical structure of the cities. In fact, in Slovenia it was especially the 20th century that created the powerful physical expression of the cities and architectural works which in turn gave rise to new traditions that were absolutely decisive for the cultural and architectural heritage of the nation. With regard to this subject several recent works are particularly interesting: the France-Bevk-Library in Nova Gorica by Ravnikar-Potokar, characterized by the complexity of its spatial composition and layout concept; the cemetery of Srebrniče by Vodopivec with its sophisticated conceptualism; the elegant details at the Linde-building by the Vozlič studio – all remarkable approaches creating a symbiosis between the perceptive experience of the works of early masters and new architectural language.

The tradition of the 20th century – i.e. the tradition that founded architectural culture in this country – is not, however, a subject with which all representatives of new Slovenian architecture want to get involved. The great "achievements" of the generation of Edvard Ravnikar as well as the intelligent compositional work on the most varied challenges of architecture or on the expressive force of the structure of buildings, the subtle spatial and town planning works by Jože Plečnik, the assimilation of regionalist approaches of some of the architecture of the 60s – are subjects that are rarely investigated by today's generations. On the contrary: the

Die Tradition des 20. Jahrhunderts – also jene, die die architektonische Kultur in diesem Land begründet hat – ist allerdings kein Thema der Auseinandersetzung für alle Vertreter der neueren slowenischen Architektur. Die großen „Errungenschaften" der Generation von Edvard Ravnikar sowie die kluge kompositorische Arbeit über die verschiedenen Skalen der Architektur oder über die Ausdruckskraft der Struktur der Gebäude, die subtilen räumlichen und städtebaulichen Arbeiten von Jože Plečnik, das Aufgreifen regionalistischer Ansätze eines Teils der Architektur der 60er Jahre – das sind Themen, die heute kaum untersucht werden. Im Gegenteil: Die Verherrlichung der funktionalen Komponente des Projekts, der beinahe obsessive Einsatz des Organisationsdiagramms, die Dominanz der Arbeit zu Umriss und Hülle zeigen vor allem internationale Bezüge. Und doch handelt es sich nicht um einen völlig unkritisch-transitiven Import. Wie die zahlreichen realisierten Projekte zeigen, befassen sich die jungen slowenischen Architekten auch mit Themen des materiellen Ausdrucks, einige mit dem Aufarbeiten ruraler Architektur, mit der Untersuchung von räumlichen Beziehungen zur Umgebung: In diesen Thematiken der Begegnung mit der Vergangenheit erweist es sich – wenn auch auf eine noch sehr zurückhaltende Art – dass die Beziehung zur Tradition ein kommender Weg ist, eine noch vollkommen offene Frage. Diese architektonische Kultur hat das Potenzial, einen sehr wertvollen persönlichen Beitrag zur internationalen Szene zu leisten – mit einem Schwerpunkt auf neue *periphere* Kulturen im Allgemeinen, die endlich beginnen, aus dem ewigen kritischen *Käfig* des Lokalismus der Vergangenheit auszubrechen.

124

glorification of the functional component, the almost obsessive use of the diagrams, the dominant role of work on the shape and skin of the buildings clearly reveal international references. And yet it is not a completely uncritical and transitive import. As the numerous completed projects show, young Slovenian architects also deal with the physical expressiveness of a building, some with the reappraisal of rural architecture, with the investigation of spatial relationships to the environment: these encounters with the past reveal – even though still in a very moderate way – that the relationship to tradition "is one of the architectural topics of the immediate future", a still entirely unwritten chapter. This architectural culture has the potential to make a very valuable personal contribution to the international scene – with a focus on new "peripheral" cultures in general which are finally beginning to break out of the eternal "critical" cage of localism attributed to them in the past.

Edvard Ravnikar
Tankstellenüberdachung
Filling station
Ljubljana 1969

Bevk-Perović
Kongresszentrum Brdo
errichtet aus Anlass der slowenischen
EU-Präsidentschaft | Congress Centre
built on the occasion of the EU presidency
Brdo pri Kranju 2005–07

Arhitektura Krušec
Aufbahrungskapelle Friedhof Teharje
Chappel Teharje cemetry
Celje 2005–07

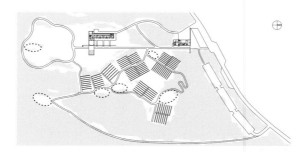

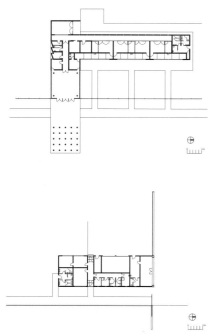

TOWARDS A GENERATION WITHOUT A MASTER

Vojteh Ravnikar
Büro- und Wohngebäude
Office and residential building
Koper 1994–96

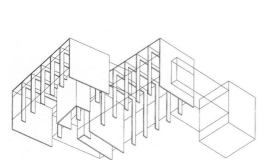

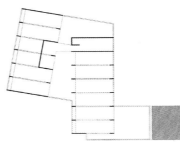

Jurij Kobe, Milena Todorič Toplišek
Krankenpflegeschule |
secondary school of nursing
Ljubljana 1995–98

Vojteh Ravnikar, Robert Potokar, Maruša Zorec
Öffentliche Bibliothek France Bevk
Public Library France Bevk
Novo Gorica 1995–2000

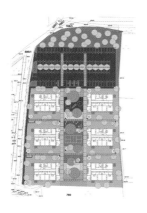

Bevk-Perović
Sozialwohnbau | social housing Polje
Ljubljana-Polje 2002–05

Ofis
Wohnhaus | housing
Bohinjska bistrica 2006–07

IN RICHTUNG EINER GENERATION OHNE MEISTER

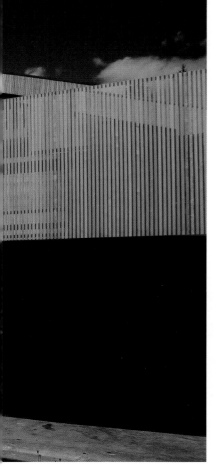

Bevk-Perović
Studentenheim | student housing
Ljubljana 2004–06

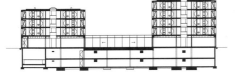

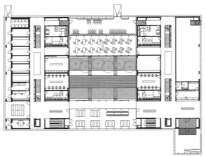

134

Sadar Vuga
Handelskammer Sloweniens
Chamber of Commerce and Industry
of Slovenia
Ljubljana 1996–99

Bevk-Perović
Haus Blejec | Blejec House
Ljubljana-Črnuče 2002–04

Sadar Vuga
Erweiterung der Nationalgalerie
National Gallery extension
Ljubljana 1996–2001

138

Sadar Vuga
„Arcadia"
Büro- und Ausstellungsgebäude
Office building and showroom
Ljubljana 1999–2001

Boris Podrecca, Miha Dobrin
Hotel Mons
Ljubljana 2004

Nande Korpnik
Büro- und Wohnhaus Maksimilijan
Office and Residential Building Maksimilijan
Celje 2005

Andrej Kemr
Touristeninformation
Tourist information center
Laško 2000

Matej Vozlič, Vesna Vozlič
Linde MPA Bürogebäude
Office building
Ljubljana 2002

Maruša Zorec, Maša Živec
Bibliothek Franc Sušnik | library Franc Sušnik
Ravne na Koroškem 2001–04

Janez Koželj, Jože Jaki
Freizeit- und Geschäftszentrum
Amusement and Commercial Center Portoval
Novo Mesto 2002–03

A.biro, Spacelab
Wohn- und Geschäftsgebäude | residential and commercial building
Ljubljana 2003–06

Zadravec Arhitekti
Höhere Schule | secondary school
Ptuj 1999–2000

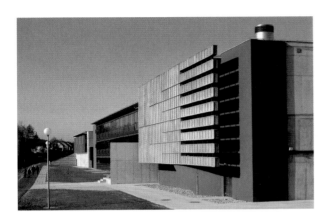

Arhitektura Krušec
Berghotel | alpine hotel "Celjska koča"
Pečovnik (Celje) 2004–06

Bevk-Perović
Königlich Niederländische Botschaft, Wohnhaus
Royal Dutch Embassy, residence
Ljubljana 2002–03

Nande Korpnik
Haus Acman | Acman House
Griže pri Žalcu 1997–99

Ofis (Rok Oman, Spela Videčnik)
„Hayrack" Wohnbau | residential building
Cerklje 2005–07

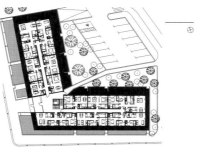

Vurnik Ivan	Kooperative Handelsbank | Cooperative Commercial Bank	1921–22	Ljubljana	Milkošičeva ul. 8
Vurnik Ivan	Sokol-Turnhalle | Sokol gymnastic hall	1923–27	Ljubljana	Tabor square
Plečnik Jože	Wechselseitige Versicherung | The Mutual Assurance Building	1928–30	Ljubljana	Milkošičeva ul. 19
Plečnik Jože	Drei Brücken und Markthallen | Tromostovje (Triple Bridge) and the Market	1929–32, 1939–44	Ljubljana	
Šubic Vladimir	„Wolkenkratzer" (Nebotičnik) | The Skyscraper (Nebotičnik)	1930–33	Ljubljana	Štefanova ulica 1–5
Plečnik Jože	National- und Universitätsbibliothek | National and University Library	1931–41	Ljubljana	Gosposka ul. 14
Dev Aleksander	Drava-Versicherung | Business Insurance Cooperative Drava	1937–40	Maribor	Ulica Talcev/Mariborska ul.
Ravnikar Edvard	Galerie der Moderne | The Museum of Modern Art	1939–51	Ljubljana	Prešernova cesta
Černigoj Jaroslav, **Dev** Aleksander	Drava-Sparkasse | The Drava Province Savings Bank	1930–31	Maribor	Tyrševa ul. 2
Šubic Vladimir	„Grafika"-Gebäude | „Grafika" Building	1937	Ljubljana	Milkošičeva/Slomškova ul.
Šubic Vladimir	Wohnhof Meksika | Meksika Apartment Complex	1926–27	Ljubljana	Njegoševa ul. 10
Mušič Vladimir	„Roter Wohnhof" | Red House Apartment Complex	1927–29	Ljubljana	Poljanska cesta 15
Hus Herman	„Kleiner Wolkenkratzer" | "Small Skyscraper"	1931–32	Ljubljana	Igriška 3
Černigoj Jaroslav, **Dev** Aleksander	Hutters Wohnblock | Hutter's Housing Block	1939–41	Maribor	Razlagova ul./ Prešernova ul.
Plečnik Jože	Christi-Himmelfahrtskirche | Parish Church of the Ascension	1924–27, 1950–56	Bogojina	Bogojina
Plečnik Jože	Franziskanerkirche | Church of St. Francis	1925–31	Ljubljana	Verovškova ul.
Plečnik Jože	Michaelskirche im Laibacher Moor | Church of St. Michael in the Marsh	1925, 1937–38	Ljubljana–Barje	Črna vas 48
Plečnik Jože	Friedhof Žale | Žale cemetery	1936–40	Ljubljana	Žale
Tomažič France	Villa Oblak	1931–35	Ljubljana	Rakovniška ul. 5
Costaperaria Josip	Villen in der Levstikova-Str. und Wohnblock „Schachbrett" | Villas in the Levstikova street and Chessboard Apartment Building	1929–32	Ljubljana	Levstikova ul./Vrtača
Strenar Maks	Villa Maria Vera	1929	Ljubljana	Cesta na Rožnik 8
Rohrman Stanislav	Villa Neuberger	1930–31	Ljubljana	Vilharjeva ul. 21
Tomažič France	Villa Grivec	1934–36	Ljubljana	Cimpermanova ul. 4
Costaperaria Josip	Villa Perhavec		Ljubljana	
Ravnikar Edvard	Revolutionsplatz (heute Republiksplatz) | Trg Revolucije	1960–82	Ljubljana	Trg Republike
Simčič Branko, **Mihelič** Milan, **Arnautović** Ilija	Messegelände, Halle A | Commercial Exhibition Grounds Hall A	1954–58	Ljubljana	Dunajska 18
Šlajmer Marko	Pavillion | Stand E–„Jurček"	1960	Ljubljana	
Mihelič Milan	Messegelände, Halle C | Commercial Exhibition Grounds Hall C	1965–67	Ljubljana	
Medvešček Emil, **Jugovec** Oton	Hauptsitz der Gewerkschaft | Headquarters of the Main Cooperative Association	1953–55	Ljubljana	Slovenska cesta/ Argentinski park
Mihevc Edo	Impex-Gebäude | Impex Building	1953–57	Ljubljana	Beethovnova ul. 11
Spinčič Ivo	Festspielhalle | Festival Hall	1960–61	Bled	Cesta svobode 11
Ravnikar Edvard	Stadthalle | Municipal Hall	1954–60	Kranj	Slovenski trg 1
Ravnikar Edvard	Slowenische Nationalbank | National Bank of Slovenia	1959–62	Kranj	Slovenski trg 2
Bonča Miloš	Geschäftsgebäude in Šiška | bommercial building in Šiška	1960–64	Ljubljana	Celovška 111
Sever Savin	Astra-Hochhaus und Bürogebäude | Astra and Commerce Towers	1963–70	Ljubljana	Dunajska 47–53
Sever Savin	Kaufhaus Merkur | Merkur Department Store	1968–70	Ljubljana	Dunajska

Ravnikar Edvard	Hotel Creina	1968–70	Kranj	Koroška cesta 5	
Mihelič Milan	Tower S2 und MATC-Gebäude | Tower S2 and MATC Building	1972–78	Ljubljana	Trg OF, Slovenska	
Mihevc Edo	„Kozolec" Wohnanlage | residential building	1953–57	Ljubljana	Dunajska	
Lajovic Janez	Hotel Prisank	1961–62	Kranjska Gora	Borovška 93	
Kristl Stanko	Kindergarten Mladi rod	1972	Ljubljana		
Furst Danilo	Volksschule | primary school	1954–59	Stražišče pri Kranju	Šolska ul. 2	
Mihelič Milan	Einkaufszentrum | Modne hiša and Prehrana Department Store	1963–67	Osijek (Hr)		
Mihelič Milan	Kaufhaus | Stoteks Department Store	1968–72	Novi Sad (Ser)		
Sever Savin	Druckerei und Verlag | Mladinska knjiga Printing House	1966	Ljubljana	Dunajska 123	
Sever Savin	Technisches Überprüfungszentrum AMZS | Technical Center of AMZS	1967–68	Ljubljana	Dunajska 128	
Jugovec Oton	Atomreaktor | Nuclear reactor of the Jožef Štefan Institute	1960–66	Podgorica		
Jugovec Oton	Rog–Baza 20	1986–88	Kočevski Rog		
Ravnikar Edvard	Gedenkstätte Konzentrationslager Kampor | Kampor Concentration Camp Memorial	1953	Insel / Island Rab (Hr) Kampor		
Ravnikar Edvard	Memorial Begunje		Begunje		
Ravnikar Edvard	Memorial Draga, Vojščica				
Ravnikar Edvard	Wohn- und Geschäftsgebäude Ferantgarten | Ferantov vrt Residential and Buisness Complex	1964–73	Ljubljana	Gregorčičeva/Rimska	
Mihelič Milan	Wohnbau | apartment building	1969–71	Ljubljana	Kersnikova	
Jugovec Oton	Villa Repotočnik	1969–78	Ljubljana	Pot na Golovec 2	
Vodopivec Aleš	Friedhof | Srebrniče Cemetery	1989, 1998–2000	Novo Mesto	Srebrniče	
Ravnikar Vojteh	Büro- und Wohngebäude | office and residential building	1994–96	Koper	Ferraska ulica 5B	
Kobe Jurij, **Todorič** Toplišek	Milena Schule | school	1995–98	Ljubljana	Poljanska cesta 61	
Ravnikar Vojteh, **Potokar** Robert, **Maruša** Zorec	Öffentliche Bibliothek | Public library „France Bevk"	1995–2000	Nova Gorica	Trg Edvarda Kardelja 4	
Bevk-Perović	Haus Blejec | Blejec House	2002–04	Ljubljana–Črnuče	Pot v smrečje 28a	
Bevk-Perović	Sozialer Wohnbau | Housing Polje	2002–05	Ljubljana–Polje	Polje 331–337	
Ofis arhitekti	Wohnbau | Housing Bohinjska bistrica	2006–07	Bohinjska Bistrica		
Bevk-Perović	Studentenwohnanlage | Student housing	2004–06	Ljubljana	Poljanska 57	
Sadar Vuga	Slowenische Handelskammer | Chamber of Commerce of Slovenia	1996–99	Ljubljana	Dimičeva 13	
Sadar Vuga	Erweiterung der Nationalgalerie | The National Gallery extension	1996–01	Ljubljana	Prešernova cesta 24	
Sadar Vuga	Büro- und Ausstellungsgebäude „Arcadia" | office building and showroom "Arcadia"	1999–01	Ljubljana	Tržaška cesta 222	
Podrecca Boris, **Dobrin** Miha	Hotel Mons	2004	Ljubljana	Pot za Brdom 55	
Korpnik Nande	Büro- und Wohngebäude | Office and Residential Building „Maksimilijan"	2005	Celje	Ljubljanska cesta	
Kemr Andrej	Touristen-Information | Tourist information center	2000	Laško	Trg svobode 8	
Vozlič Matej, **Vozlič** Vesna	Gebäude der Linde MPA | office builiding	2002	Ljubljana	Vodovodna cesta 99	
Enota	Hotel Sotelia	2004–06	Podčetrtek	Zdraviliška c. 24	

Max Fabiani 1865–1962

Jože Plečnik 1872–1957

Josip Costaperaria 1876–1951

Ivan Vurnik 1884–1971

Vladimir Šubic 1894–1946

Herman Hus 1896–1960

Dušan Grabrijan 1899–1952

France Tomažič 1899–1968

Miroslav Oražem 1900–1975

Franc Novak 1906–1959

Edvard Ravnikar 1907–1993

Marjan Tepina 1913–2004

Hrvoje Brnčič 1914–1991

Marko Župančič 1914–2007

Jovan Krunić 1915–2001

Savin Sever 1927–2003